THE NORTH EAST
& YORKSHIRE

EXPLORING WOODLAND

WOODLAND
TRUST

THE NORTH EAST
& YORKSHIRE

Edited by Graham Blight

FRANCES LINCOLN LIMITED
PUBLISHERS

Acknowledgements

Introduction by Archie Miles
Site entries written by Sheila Ashton
Researched by Tim Hill, Diana Moss & Lorraine Weeks.
Edited by Graham Blight
Maps by Linda M Dawes, Belvoir Cartographics & Design
Regional maps created using Maps in Minutes data ©MAPS IN MINUTES™/
Collins Bartholomews 2007
Site maps © Woodland Trust

Photographic acknowledgements
Forestry Commission: 31; Foto 45/Stuart Handley: 106, 108, 110
NTPL/Andrea Jones: 21; NTPL/Nick Meers: 42
WTPL: 1 (David Lund), 2 (Kenneth Watkins), 8 (Keith Huggett), 11, 14 (David Lund),
20 (Dave Foker), 27 (Keith Huggett), 34, 36 (Keith Huggett), 38 (Kenneth Watkins), 40,
46 (Gary Haley), 47, 51 (Gary Haley), 52 (M. Peckett), 54, 63, 69, 70 (James Simpson),
73, 82 (David Lund), 83 (Jon Parsons), 85 (Ian Gilkison), 88 (Tessa Bunney), 97 (Simon
Clark), 115 (Ian Edwards), 116 (David Lund), 121, 123 (Keith Huggett)

Frances Lincoln Ltd
4 Torriano Mews
Torriano Avenue
London NW5 2RZ
www.franceslincoln.com

The North East & Yorkshire
Copyright © Frances Lincoln 2008
Text © Woodland Trust 2008
Maps © see above

First Frances Lincoln edition: 2008

A catalogue record for this book is available
from the British Library.

ISBN 978-0-7112-2666-1

Printed and bound in Singapore
The paper used in this book was sourced from
sustainable forests, managed according to FSC
(Forest Stewardship Council) guidelines.

1 2 3 4 5 6 7 8 9

Half title page Lower Grass Wood

Title page Nunsbrough Wood

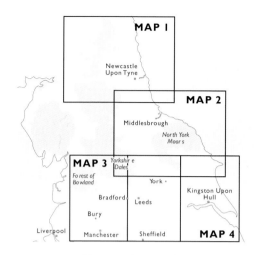

MAP I

Newcastle
Upon Tyne

MAP 2

Middlesbrough

North York
Moors

MAP 3 Yorkshire
Dales

Forest of
Bowland

York •

Kingston Upon
Hull

Bradford

Leeds

Bury

Liverpool   Sheffield

Manchester   MAP 4

Contents

How to use this guide

Covering a region that encompasses Yorkshire and the North East, this book is divided into four areas represented by key maps on pages 16–17, 48–49, 78–79 and 104–105. The tree symbols on these maps denote the location of each wood. In the pages following the key maps, the sites nearest one another are described together (wherever practical) to make planning a day out as rewarding as possible.

For each site entry the name of the nearest town/village is given, followed by road directions and the grid reference of the site entrance. The area of the site (in hectares followed by acres) is given together with the official status of the site where appropriate and the owner, body or organisation responsible for maintaining the site. Symbols are used to denote information about the site and its facilities as explained in the next column.

Type of wood

Mainly broadleaved woodland

Mainly coniferous woodland

Mixed woodland

Car park

Parking on site

Parking nearby

Parking difficult to find

Official status

Area of Outstanding Natural Beauty
AONB

Site of Special Scientific Interest SSSI

Site facilities

Sign at entry

Information board

One or more paths suitable for
 wheelchair users

Dogs allowed under supervision

Waymarked trail

Toilet

Picnic area

Entrance/car park charge

Refreshments on site

The North East & Yorkshire

Hartburn Glebe

'Don't go too close. Be careful. Hold my hand tightly.' My mother's anxiety recalled today as strongly as the clammy protective hand that kept me firmly away from trouble. My Yorkshire childhood brings back many fond memories, but none sweeter than those with a hint of danger. Balmy summer day trips in The Dales; chugging happily through the countryside in my grandma's peacock blue Morris 1000. One of our favourite days out was Bolton Abbey, skimming stones across the river, on to The Strid for a picnic lunch, and then tea and buns at Barden Tower.

The Strid certainly stuck in the mind more for its hazardous reputation than its glorious woodland setting. Here the tumbling waters of the river Wharfe are suddenly constricted by a narrow gritstone passage, not only very deep, but also undercut with many ledges beneath the surface. The estate brochure warns of the dangers of trying to jump the river here – '. . . remember that anything that goes into The Strid rarely surfaces for several days.'

The forces of nature are formidable, but that said The Strid and its attendant woodlands with their excellent network of paths have been a lure for visitors for almost 200 years. In many respects this wood is typical of many other ancient woodlands in Yorkshire that have survived in the deeper, narrower valleys, where they have been safe from the marauding grazings of sheep and too inaccessible for agricultural improvement.

Around some of the larger cities such as Sheffield, Leeds and Bradford a handful of quite sizeable woods have endured mainly because they had some economic association with the city industries. An abundance of coppice woods, known in this region as 'spring woods', were constantly required to provide charcoal, tan bark, fuel wood and timber. Hetchell Wood, near Leeds, typifies many of these woodlands of the acidic gritstones with predominantly sessile oak and birch growing from a carpet of heaths, bilberry and bracken. Since most of these woods are no longer rigorously managed, occasional plantings such as beech or blow-ins such as sycamore have added to the mix. Sycamore is a great coloniser, a pretty good habitat for many insects (plus the birds these attract), and a provider of excellent timber.

Understanding exactly how these woodlands have evolved all adds to the fascination, and this is merely one aspect of a wonderful woodland project currently under way near Bradford. The Royds Community Association, at Wyke, have put together one of the very best booklets dedicated to a single woodland that I've had the pleasure to read. Judy Woods is more than a single wood; in reality a group of several adjoining woods which line the Royds Hall Beck. The booklet takes you on a ramble through the history and evolution of the woods, laced with anecdotal tales of some of the colourful characters who frequented them. Judy Woods derives from Judy North who, in the 19th century, lived in the woods and sold 'sticks of spice, parkin pigs and ginger beer' to the many visitors. There are also tales of buried treasure and 'ghostly goings on' in the wood, much concerning its industrial past, as well as interpretation of the existing woodland structure and wildlife, and even a management strategy for the future. What more could you ask for?

Projects like this are so crucial in urban areas where a true empathy with woodland and an appreciation of its huge importance as a wildlife habitat can be nurtured within the community.

On the other side of the Leeds/Bradford conurbation a somewhat different urban woodland experience awaits. A few minutes from the dual carriageway of the A63, as it roars eastwards out of Leeds, lies the Temple Newsam Estate. Here, much of the woodland is in small, well-managed stands or clumps of fine specimen trees, which hark back to its 18th century landscaped heyday. The house is frequently used for fairs or functions. There are formal gardens, lakeside walks and loads of open space to play games, picnic or just snooze in the sun. A working farm, farm museum and rare breeds centre are also a great attraction for children. Yet again these old estates prove their supreme value as both marvellous amenities and green oases amidst the cut and thrust of city life.

Farther north and the Dales country is regained once more. In the upper reaches, where limestone prevails, some startling little woods adorn the deep cut gorges and gills, and few more spectacular than Thornton and Twisleton Glens above Ingleton. Torrents of water rushing off the fells have carved through the different types of rock forming giant steps over which dramatic falls cascade – Thornton Force perhaps the most impressive of all. Oak is the dominant tree here, with alder and willow along the waterside. The urban Victorians loved to explore wild and rugged countryside, and in the latter part of the 19th century a fast-expanding rail system was eager to transport them to their rural idyll. In 1885 the most astute folks of Ingleton set up an 'improvement company' to build paths, construct bridges and provide seats along a Waterfall Walk. Visitors came in their thousands, and have kept coming to marvel ever since.

The landscape of this western reach of Yorkshire contrasts sharply with the softer undulating folds of the Yorkshire Wolds and the North York Moors in the east. In this more open countryside some of the largest tracts of woodland in Yorkshire are encountered, albeit much of it heavily coniferised. An unforgettable approach to the North York Moors from the west, takes the steep snaking road up Sutton Bank on to the Hambleton Hills (watch out for low-flying

St Ives Estate

gliders). At the top a National Park Visitor Centre makes a grand starting point for numerous bridleways and paths, notably the long distance Cleveland Way. The 'nature trail' path drops down into Garbutt Wood, which nestles between the thousand-foot crags of Whitestone Cliff and an ancient lake with the spooky name of Gormire, believed to be a relic of the last ice age. Bluebells make a great show in springtime, but the stars here are the splendid old gnarled oaks and birches.

However, if it's truly ancient oaks you want to see then Duncombe Park, near the small market town of Helmsley, is the place to be. This fine ancestral home is surrounded by parkland largely created in the 18th century, which fortunately managed to employ much of the existing ancient wood-pasture into the schemes of that time. English Nature look after the most sensitive parts of the site and permission must be sought to visit these areas which could not cope so well with mass visitor pressure. Here the vast crumbling oak pollards are many hundreds of years old and the site is considered one of the most important in northern England for wood–feeding insects. The more formal parts of the parkland contain some equally spectacular specimen trees, such as the tallest common lime in Britain at a majestic 44 metres (144 feet 4 inches).

Nearby Bridestones Moor, in the Dalby Forest, harbours some gargantuan rock formations, known locally as nabs, which Gerald Wilkinson once so aptly described as, 'Jurassic vol-au-vents of perhaps 200 tons apiece made by the giant Pastry Cook 150 million years ago.' These strange outcrops of sandstone are composed of a mixture of hard and soft layers which have been sculpted by wind, rain and frost erosion. Most of the surrounding woodland is part of a vast conifer plantation begun in 1919, but the Forestry Commission has now instigated new regimes to vary the tree age within stands, break up solid ranks of trees and encourage some of the smaller enclaves of broadleaves. Proof positive that these hills were once cloaked in a rich broadleaf mix has come from excavations of New Stone Age burial mounds here, beneath which the 5,000 year old remains of woodlands, once cleared for agriculture, have been detected.

For an altogether different view of the moors take a trip on the North York Moors Railway and steam sedately from Pickering to Grosmont along one of the finest scenic lines in the land. Alternatively, dovetail a round trip on part of the railway with a good walk and a pint at one of the many fine hostelries around the moor.

The salt-laden northeast coast of Yorkshire wouldn't appear to be very promising for woodlands, but tucked in some of the valleys a few gems await discovery. Mulgrave Woods, near Sandsend, lines two valleys on a private estate, where 200 years of management and artistry have created something special. Humphry Repton was brought in for a makeover (how did he fit it all in, travelling the length and breadth of the country?). His legacy? Some wonderful vistas, decorative stone bridges and a rock tunnel, much of which is currently being restored to the original vision. The woodland is a healthy mixture of hard and softwoods, and seasonal delights include carpets of snowdrops, primroses and bluebells, as well as stunning autumn colours.

A little further up the coast, at Saltburn-by-the-Sea, there's another fine coastal valley woodland, so if it's too blustery for a walk on the front or too nippy for a dip in the briny, try a walk through Rifts Wood in the Saltburn Valley – a fairly small wood with lots of year round interest and an excellent Woodland Centre, ideal for families and schools.

Rifts Wood is a very small part of a network of woodlands, both new and old, which have been designated as part of the Tees Forest, one of England's twelve Community Forests, which wraps its green way around the lower Tees valley. The other Community Forest within this region is the Great North Forest in County Durham and Tyneside. The aims of these forests are broadly similar; by planting anew and by better management of existing trees and woodland the main thrust is a greening of some of the more environmentally ravaged or neglected regions around urban conurbations and industrialised communities, and by revitalising these landscapes, making them healthier and more pleasant places to live, work and play. The maturing forests will have both commercial and amenity value, and greatly improve habitat potential for wildlife.

On the northern tip of the Tees Forest lies Castle Eden Dene; a designated National Nature Reserve, at 222 hectares (549 acres) this is the largest area of ancient woodland in the north east. Twelve miles of paths weave through this deep four-mile gorge as it cuts through the Magnesian limestone towards the sea. Yews, which love the calcareous rocks grow here in profusion making a marvellous contrasting backdrop for the bright springtime foliage of the dominant ash. This is a superb site for wildlife – 300 different fungi are known to grow here and some 3000 species of insect, although there are likely to be even more than this. Better still perhaps is the thought that you may well see red squirrels scampering through the trees. Yet another of those public spirited Victorian clergymen, Rev. John Burdon, must be acknowledged for creating carriageways, footpaths and footbridges which originally opened up this magical place to visitors.

A stark contrast with the rugged gorge woodlands are those legacies of the golden age of landscaping, when trees and woodland were but two strings to the grand designer's bow. Gibside, in the Derwent valley, has all the trees you could desire, both natives and

Bilton Beck

exotics, plus a Palladian Chapel, Column of Liberty, Orangery, Walled Garden and Banqueting House.... oh yes, and some romantic ruins; and all this is very handy if you live in the Newcastle metropolis.

Northumberland contains woods on contrasting scales. While the country's largest wooded forest is to be found at Kielder, three quarters of the county's other woods are less than ten hectares in size. However, amongst these there are some great little woods and, as expected, they're often found in steep secluded valleys.

West of Hexham find the Allen Valley with its network of interlinked woods; Allen Banks, Staward Gorge and Briarwood Banks. Exploring this valley will unearth the remains of a medieval pele tower and gatehouse, evidence of coal and lead mining and three lime kilns. There's a manmade network of 'Wilderness Walks' created between 1830 and 1860, with suspension bridges spanning the torrent below. A wide variety of native broadleaves are present as well as planted beech and conifers. There's an unusual floral treasure to be found in a meadow where wild pansies beam brightly from the sward amongst a stand of conifers, and you may care to know (although you'll be very lucky to see one) that this is the northernmost habitat for the dormouse.

Closer to Hexham a heartwarming springtime picture awaits at Letah Wood, near Newbiggin, where a fine show of wild daffodils makes the woodland floor glow. This is thought to be the last stronghold in Northumberland of these dainty little flowers of ancient woodland.

For flowers of an altogether more overpowering nature look no further than the banks of rhododendrons at Cragside, a National Trust property near Rothbury, where house and garden were the creations of the first Lord Armstrong, a great Victorian innovator and industrialist. A grand day out for families here, with walks aplenty, formal gardens to admire, an adventure playground and, of course, an excellent cafe and shop. Cragside holds a special place in history as the first house in the world to have been lit by hydroelectricity, and the lakes at the top of the estate, as well as the waterwheel that they powered, can all still be seen. A superb collection of trees combines impressive native specimens with a host of conifers from around the world, either set within the rugged natural landscape or adorning some of the dramatic man-made vistas.

A complete contrast, far from the company of others in one of the remotest parts of Northumberland, is a day spent exploring the College valley, not far from Wooler. This great open space beneath the Cheviot Hills offers purple heather-clad moors, little white farmsteads dotting the landscape, and woodlands either of conifers or, along the valley sides, fragments of ancient broadleaf. This is wild and woolly country where you must keep your wits about you – no bears or wolves here (yet), but the weather can sometimes take a turn for the worse quite rapidly, so set out well equipped and well informed.

The northeast of England may not be the most wooded area of Britain, and even though many of the finest woods may seem remote or inaccessible, they most definitely reward those with the desire and energy to seek them out, and once discovered they will prove a source of pleasure at any time of year.

ARCHIE MILES

MAP 1

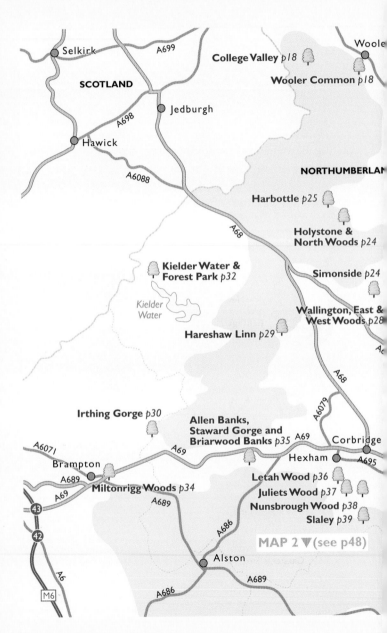

Selkirk

A699

College Valley p18

Wooler

SCOTLAND

Wooler Common p18

Jedburgh

A698

Hawick

A6088

NORTHUMBERLAND

Harbottle p25

A68

Holystone &
North Woods p24

Kielder Water &
Forest Park p32

Simonside p24

Kielder
Water

Wallington, East &
West Woods p28

Hareshaw Linn p29

A68

A6079

A68

Irthing Gorge p30

Allen Banks,
Staward Gorge and
Briarwood Banks p35

A69

Corbridge

A6071

A69

Hexham

A695

Brampton

A689

Letah Wood p36

A69

Miltonrigg Woods p34

Juliets Wood p37

43

A689

Nunsbrough Wood p38

Slaley p39

42

A686

MAP 2 ▼ (see p48)

A6

Alston

M6

A689

A686

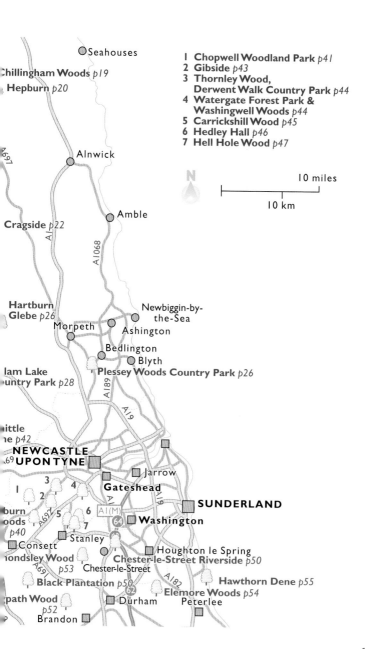

O Seahouses

Chillingham Woods *p19*

Hepburn *p20*

1 **Chopwell Woodland Park** *p41*
2 **Gibside** *p43*
3 **Thornley Wood,**
  Derwent Walk Country Park *p44*
4 **Watergate Forest Park &**
  Washingwell Woods *p44*
5 **Carrickshill Wood** *p45*
6 **Hedley Hall** *p46*
7 **Hell Hole Wood** *p47*

Alnwick

N

10 miles

10 km

Amble

Cragside *p22*

A1068

Hartburn
Glebe *p26*

Morpeth

Newbiggin-by-
the-Sea

Ashington

Bedlington

O Blyth

Plessey Woods Country Park *p26*

lam Lake
untry Park *p28*

A189

A19

ittle
e *p42*

NEWCASTLE
UPON TYNE

3
4

1

2

Jarrow

Gateshead

burn
oods
p40

5

6

7

SUNDERLAND

A1(M)

64

Washington

Consett

Stanley

Houghton le Spring

iondsley Wood

Chester-le-Street Riverside *p50*

p53

Chester-le-Street

A182

Hawthorn Dene *p55*

Black Plantation *p50*

62

Elemore Woods *p54*

path Wood
p52

Durham

Peterlee

Brandon

17

MAP 1

College Valley
Wooler

Follow A697 north from Wooler take B6351 west towards Kirknewton. After Kirknewton take minor road left at Westnewton towards Hethpool. Follow road until cattle grid. Park in field at beginning of College Valley. Use of road beyond car park by permit only. (NT895285)
4800 ha (11864 acres) SSSI
College Valley Estates Ltd.

Stamina and determination pay dividends for visitors to College Valley in Northumberland National Park.

The best way to explore this beautiful landscape is to arrive early and spend all day walking, cycling or riding along its 28-mile web of footpaths and bridleways.

The woodland, surrounded by the bold, dramatic landscape of the Cheviot Hills, rises 2282 ft from Hethpool Lakes to the summit of Cheviot.

This valley of contrasts has many different habitats, colours and textures set beneath rapidly changing skies. Scattered conifer plantations cloak parts of the hillside with deciduous woodland, heather moorland, swathes of bracken and farmland painting a patchwork on the landscape. College Burn, heavily camouflaged by scrub, runs through the centre of the valley.

It is worth noting that because of rapid weather changes, visitors are recommended to leave route details in their car.

Wooler Common
Wooler

Heading south on A697 (South Road) turn right into The Perth. Turn left into Ramsey Lane which continues into Common Road. Woods and car park on right. Brown tourist signs from A697 and town centre. (NT980277)
81 ha (200 acres)
Forestry Commission

Wooler Common Woodland Park, in the heart of the Cheviot Hills, has a wild beauty that masks a turbulent history.

An open common, it is enveloped by well managed community woodland where standard trees are planted as tributes to local people.

Marauding Scots targeted the area between the 14th and 16th centuries but it is on the common that most historical evidence remains. The relics of a hill top fort stand close to Pin Well, where young ladies would make a wish for love on May Day. Overlooking it is the King's Chair, a rocky outcrop where a Scottish king is said to have observed a battle and from where visitors can enjoy more stunning – but serene – views of the surrounding countryside.

The site is crisscrossed by a network of well-maintained paths and there are two trails, one wheelchair-friendly route, dotted with willow sculptures, that circles Humbleton Burn where wildfowl can be spotted on two ponds.

Chillingham Woods
Chillingham

Follow A697 south taking B6348 left at Wooler. At the village of Chatton take right towards Chillingham. Along this road turn off left to Chillingham, woods are on the right. (NU063260)
250 ha (618 acres)

College Valley Estates Ltd

If you want to enjoy Chillingham Woods at their best, take your time. This popular local beauty spot is to savour. Keep your ears and eyes open as you explore as it is bursting with wildlife.

As you tread carefully among the mixed conifer and broadleaf woodland, look for signs of roe and fallow deer, red squirrels, foxes, badgers and hares, which all thrive here. It is also possible to spot birds such as buzzard, green and great spotted woodpecker, goshawk, nuthatch and even crossbill.

The woodland sits within the stunning landscape of the Cheviots in north Northumberland, not too far from the Scottish border and is perfect for walkers who can enjoy a series of waymarked routes through the site.

While you won't be able to spy the fabulous famed beasts of nearby Chillingham Wild Cattle Park from the woodland, guided walks are available.

MAP 1

Hepburn
Alnwick

Follow A697 south, turning left
onto B6348 at Wooler. At the
village of Chatton take right
towards Chillingham. Go past
Chillingham and take left turn
minor road to Hepburn.
Woods are 1.6km (1 mile) on
right. (NU073248)
102 ha (252 acres)
Forestry Commission

The remains of a hill fort on
Hepburn Crag suggest the site
has been inhabited for at least
4000 years. Today, from this
natural vantage point, the
steep sandstone crags give
stunning views of the
surrounding countryside.

One of the two waymarked
routes features a replica stone-
lined grave, while the longer
leads past Berthele's Stone
which can be seen on the
ascent. A diversion to visit the
top of Ros Hill provides a
stunning viewpoint that was
once the home of one of the
Border Beacons.

Hepburn wood is a mixture
of coniferous plantation and
ancient woodland, parts of
which are over 400 years old.
Look skywards to spot circling
buzzards, be alert to roe deer
racing across the forest drive
ahead of you and, if you tread
quietly, there is always the
chance of catching sight of a
fox or a badger at dusk.

Roe deer

Cragside (see next page)

MAP 1

Cragside
Rothbury

21km (13 miles) southwest of Alnwick (B6341) and 24km (15 miles) northwest of Morpeth on Wooler road (A697), turn left on to B6341 at Moorhouse Crossroads, entrance 1.6km (1 mile) north of Rothbury. (NU073022)

400 ha (989 acres)

The National Trust

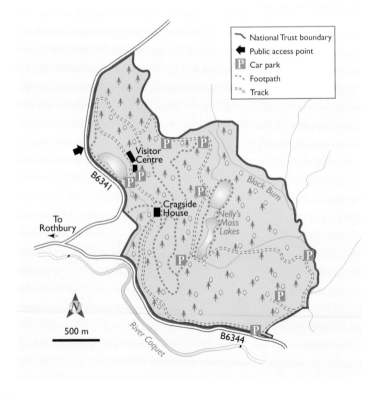

There is a huge, wild feel to Cragside, a large estate where tall trees stand among huge rock outcrops and with lots of different woodland walks to explore.

This is truly a place of wonder. It was created by the great Victorian innovator and industrialist Lord Armstrong, who transformed a bare hillside into a riot of rhododendron that blazes in full bloom during late May and June, and exotic trees.

A total of seven million trees and shrubs were planted to create the 1,000-acre forest garden that is still providing magic more than a century on.

The efforts of man and Nature combine at Cragside, with magnificent views of the estate and surrounding countryside and an impressive range of veteran trees to inspire the mind – including a Douglas fir, towering pines and formal plantings. England's tallest tree can be found in the pinetum on the estate, which can be explored via miles of footpaths and drives.

Two large lakes at the top of the estate once powered a waterwheel to provide electricity for the Victorian house – the first in the world to be lit by hydroelectricity. Described as 'the Palace of a Modern Magician', the 1880s property was well ahead of its time, with hot and cold running water, fire alarms, telephones, a Turkish bath suite and even a passenger lift.

The house is surrounded by one of Europe's largest rock gardens, while across the valley is a terraced garden where exotic fruits were nurtured year-round in glasshouses – as they are today in the Orchard House.

The estate features a six-mile drive so it is possible to get a good feel for the estate without leaving the car. Those exploring on foot are advised to wear stout footwear to enable you to tackle a series of steps and sharp gradients.

MAP 1

Simonside
Harwood

From Rothbury take B6342 south. Turn right following sign to Simonside. Follow minor road for 5km (3 miles), forest on left. (NZ037996)

2954 ha (7300 acres)

Forestry Commission

There is a wild and rugged beauty to Simonside, a mature forest rising up the dark slopes of the Simonside Hills which dominate the middle reaches of Coquetdale.

Simonside is the haunt of serious walkers but there is a fine reward for those who tackle the challenging 6.5km (4 miles) climb to Simonside Ridge where moorland birds such as red grouse and ring ouzel nestle. Here you can enjoy stunning and dramatic views of the Cheviots and, on a clear day, the entire Northumbrian coastline.

Those who don't make it to the summit can enjoy a walk through the forest by choosing one of the less-challenging waymarked routes including a 1.6km (1 mile) walk from the car park through post-World War II larch plantations.

Ravensheugh is a strenuous walk of 7 km (4.5 miles) taking a steady climb through pine plantations with silver birch and rowan, past a 4,000-year-old Bronze Age burial cairn, emerging onto open moorland.

Holystone & North Woods
Holystone Village

On the A696 south turn left near Otterburn onto B6341. Take next minor road left to Harbottle and next left to Holystone, car park on left. (NT950024)

209 ha (517 acres) SSSI

Forestry Commission

Tucked away in a quiet corner of Coquetdale you will discover the beauty, peace and tranquillity of Holystone Wood.

The village of Holystone evolved around a 12th century nunnery, now gone, but its atmosphere of remoteness can still be enjoyed with beautiful walks and a rich natural and historical heritage.

A commercial plantation, Holystone is also a popular recreation spot with contrasting landscapes and views. One moment you are in dense woodland, with lichens and mosses dripping off the trees, and the next emerging into open moorland and farmland.

Three waymarked routes vary from forest rides to challengingly muddy paths. The longest of the walks, at 8km (5 miles), leads deep into the forest plantations to Holystone Common and Dove Crags. A shorter Farm Walk skirts the ancient woodland of North Wood while the shortest of the walks follows the route of a former Roman road out onto farmland and Lady's Well.

While in the area you may like to extend your walk to include Harbottle Wood (see next entry), which adjoins Holystone.

Harbottle (West Wood)
Harbottle

On the A696 south turn left near Otterburn into B6341. Take next minor road left to Harbottle. Go through Harbottle, woods are on left. (NT927048)
599 ha (1480 acres) SSSI
Forestry Commission

The drive northwest from Rothbury to Harbottle is eye-catching, with interest increasing as you get ever closer. This may be a standard Forestry Commission plantation, divided into two – West Wood and Harbottle Wood – but is set in stunning countryside.

A hike through knee-high heather leads to the Drake Stone and Harbottle Lake. From these heights, the grandeur of the surrounding landscape can be enjoyed – rolling hills dotted with grazing sheep, plantations, heather moorland, the river Coquet carving its way through the valley below, and to the north the Upper Coquetdale Valley and the Cheviots.

A trip to nearby Lady's Well and Harbottle Castle, which are within just a couple of miles, is recommended. The southerly edge of Harbottle merges with Holystone Wood (see previous entry).

MAP 1

Plessey Woods Country Park
Bedlington

Take the A1068 south of Bedlington and wood is on right. Or, heading north from Newcastle on A1, take A19 junction then A1068 toward Ashington. Approaching Hartburn Bridge, Plessey is signed to left just after bridge. (NZ240800)
40 ha (100 acres)
Northumberland County Council

People have been flocking to Plessey Woods for generations to enjoy the woods and river. Plessey offers the chance to escape life's stresses by getting close to Nature.

Known locally as Bluebell Woods, this is the ideal place for a family day out. The woodland sustains an array of birds including the great spotted woodpecker, nuthatch and tree creeper while red squirrel, fox and roe deer also make their presence known.

The banks of the River Blyth provide a wonderful habitat for kingfishers, dippers and otters – keep alert and you might spot one.

There is a world of recreation opportunities to choose from, including fishing, riding, orienteering, cycling, canoeing and of course, walking with many self-guided trails laid out. A guide has been produced to help people with mobility difficulties get the most out of their visit. Refreshments are available from the café on site, open each weekend and school holidays.

Hartburn Glebe
Hartburn

Take B6343 turning off A1 (near Morpeth) and follow toward Cambo. The wood is on the right and there is a small lay-by at the first entrance. (NZ088864)
3 ha (8 acres)
The Woodland Trust

It is easy to see why writers have waxed lyrical about romantic Hartburn Glebe since the 18th century.

Set in an area 'of great landscape value', this beautiful wood sustains a rich variety of wildlife including red squirrels,

Hartburn Glebe

badgers and otters and an abundance of wild garlic, woodrush and yellow pimpernel.

History, as well as Nature, beckons experts and casual visitors alike to Hartburn Glebe. A deep natural hole in the stream bed on the wood's northeastern side was said to conceal silver and valuables snatched in Viking raids and the famed Roman road the Devil's Causeway crossed Hart Burn, where goosanders, heron and the occasional kingfisher are spotted today.

Another magical attraction is a wonderful Grade ll listed grotto, linked to the river by a tunnel which was adapted for the use of bathers. There is also an elaborate sandstone bridge and a series of walkways fashioned by 18th century Hartburn vicar, the Rev. Doctor Sharpe.

MAP 1

Bolam Lake
Country Park
Belsay

Signposted off A696 near Belsay.
(NZ083820)

40 ha (100 acres)

Northumberland County Council

An assortment of self-guided trails, available from the visitor centre, helps people get the most out of a day at this well-used park.

The impressive man–made 25-acre lake was created in 1818 and today attracts an impressive range of birdlife including resident mute swans. If you arrive in winter with bird food, hungry blue tits can be fed by hand in the clearings beside the car parks.

Bolam Lake Country Park caters for a range of interests. In summer, families take picnics on the meadows while others enjoy the cool shade by following a variety of woodland walks. The lake meanwhile is busy with fishermen and canoeists.

Wallington, Hartburn Glebe and Belsay Castle and Hall with its magnificent 30-acre gardens are all close by.

Wallington, East &
West Woods
Morpeth

Heading south-east on A696 turn right onto B6342 to Cambo. Follow this road for 4km (2.5 miles), wood is on left. (NZ030843)

45 ha (111 acres)

The National Trust

Venture into the heart of beautiful rural Northumberland to encounter one of the most accessible and stunning woodland sites the North East has to offer.

Wallington, East & West Woods form part of the Wallington estate, home of the Trevelyan family and full of lovely features from parkland and walled gardens, imaginative woodland sculptures and water features.

Full of changing scenery, the woods go from open parkland dotted with native and exotic species to open beech woodland followed by dense conifer plantation and regenerating ash.

East & West Woods are mixed deciduous woodlands with ponds and waterways, a good network of well-kept footpaths and seating where visitors can enjoy peaceful rests. A wildlife hide in West Wood gives a chance to spot deer, birds and red squirrels by Middle Pond.

For a really adventurous walk, follow the trails through West Wood, along the river Wansbeck and up into the walled garden, returning to the hall via East Wood.

Hareshaw Linn
Bellingham

From A69 Newcastle to Carlisle road, take A6079 west of Hexham and follow B6320 to Bellingham. Turn right after Bellingham town hall. Go down hill and over bridge. Car park on left opposite police station. (NY842846)
20 ha (49 acres) SSSI

Northumberland National Park Authority

Steeped in natural beauty and a rich industrial heritage, Hareshaw Linn is a broadleaf valley woodland with a magnificent waterfall as its focal point.

The woodland – a mixture of oak and ash with a hazel understorey and the occasional Scots pine and Douglas fir, a legacy of the Victorians, has been loved by generations of local people. An impressive 300 different mosses, lichens and liverworts thrive in the wood and can be seen cloaking the trees.

Six bridges, one of them hand-crafted, cross the Linn and add to the quality of this stunning setting. Many remnants of the former ironworks that once dominated the valley can be found and the quarry workings have left a lime-rich soil in which plants such as fairy flax are thriving.

MAP 1

Irthing Gorge
Gilsland

Either park in the village of
Gilsland and follow the public
footpath which passes Wardrew
House or turn off B6318 in
Gilsland toward Gilsland Spa.
If you can find a space to park
near the hotel you can walk into
the wood from here. (NY634685)
34 ha (84 acres) SSSI
The Woodland Trust

History, romance, spectacular
scenery, watersports and an
abundance of wildlife – Irthing
Gorge has it all.

This ancient woodland, a
Site of Special Scientific
Interest in the
Northumberland National
Park, forms part of a mosaic of
wildlife habitats. It lines the
steep sides of a deep gorge
chiselled by the fast-flowing
River Irthing. At its head is a
waterfall known as Crammel
Linn. Now the Woodland Trust
is planting native trees on
adjoining grassland to buffer
and extend the ancient
woodland.

Red squirrels and badgers
inhabit the gorge, alongside a
varied bird population and a
rich mix of woodland plants.
Yew grows on the cliff edges
while ash dominates the lower
slopes and birch is to be found
on higher ground.

The gorge lies 6.5km (4
miles) north of Gilsland, one of
19th century Britain's most
fashionable spa resorts. Still
popular, its scenery is as
romantic as ever.

Kielder Water & Forest Park (see next page)

MAP 1

Kielder Water & Forest Park
Kielder

From A69 at Hexham take A6079 north then left onto B6318 for a short distance. Follow B6320 to Bellingham, then minor road signed to Kielder. (NY632935)

60,000 ha (148,295 acres) SSSI

Forestry Commission

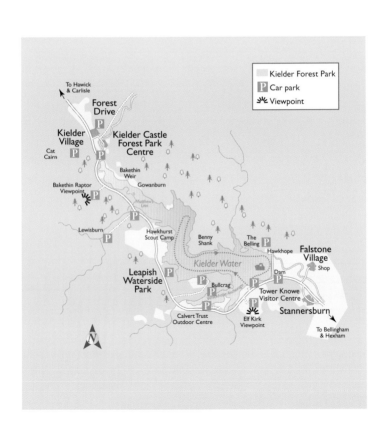

One of Britain's biggest nature resorts, vast Kielder Forest and Kielder Water is full of wild, Northern romance and magic.

Although quite remote, this enormous site is hugely popular, attracting more than a quarter of a million visitors a year, making it one of Northumberland's top five tourist attractions. But the 250-square-mile expanse is capable of absorbing the crowds. You could spend a week here without feeling crowded.

For a sense of freedom and vastness, enjoy the vistas across Kielder Water, Europe's largest man-made lake – it will fill you with awe. But the reservoir is not the only star – it shares the glory with the woodland.

If you have ever hankered to see remote working forests on a large scale, this is the place to be. Vast expanses of plantations – 150 million standing trees – can be seen at all levels of maturity within a mammoth forest producing 1,300 tonnes of timber a day.

Brimming with red squirrels, deer and birds, this giant nature reserve includes no fewer than eight designated Sites of Special Scientific Interest. The woodland is dominated by Sitka spruce and pine but there is a broadleaf presence here and with a planting programme in hand, the percentage of hardwoods on the site is expected to increase over the next decade and a half.

Size is not everything and there are ample opportunities to enjoy walks in small areas of woodland and plantations; relish the sight of ferns dripping with dew, soak in the sights of wonderful outdoor sculptures including the 'Cat Cairn' Kielder Skyspace structure, or join the children tracing fairy rings in dense, dark plantations.

Lots of routes mean lots of choice. The forest drive goes east to west through the heart of the forest and there are countless tracks for foot, horseback or cycling access. If you prefer to have your day organised, there are numerous events to choose from.

MAP 1

Miltonrigg Woods
Brampton

A69 from Brampton, turn right on
minor road heading south, car park
30m on right. (NY559612)
63 ha (157 acres)
The Woodland Trust

Just a few miles south of
historic Hadrian's Wall is a
landmark of Nature's making –
Miltonrigg Wood.

A network of paths,
including a surfaced route
suitable for visitors in
wheelchairs or with buggies,
leads you through this peaceful
ancient woodland.

Oak timber harvested from
this site is reputed to have been
used for the rebuilding of
sections of York Minster roof.
Some areas were planted with
conifers in the post-war years
and rhododendron has
dominated the wood in the
past. A programme of
restoration work aims to
return the wood to its
original character.

Miltonrigg is alive with birds
including kestrel, sparrowhawk,
tawny owl, great spotted
woodpecker, redstart and coal
tit among the more common
woodland birds. Summer
visitors might be lucky enough
to witness the evening display
flight of a woodcock.

A pond at the heart of the
wood provides a habitat for
dragonflies, toads and newts.

Miltonrigg Woods

Allen Banks, Staward Gorge & Briarwood Banks
Haydon Bridge

6.5km (4 miles) west of Haydon Bridge on the A69, turn south onto minor road signed Allen Banks. Having crossed river, take left fork and follow road to National Trust Allen Banks car park. To reach Briarwood Banks either walk along river from Allen Banks car park or follow signs to Plankey Mill and park at farm (NY791620). Cross river bridge to reserve. Staward Gorge can be accessed from either car park. (NY797640/NY791620)
200 ha (494 acres) SSSI

The National Trust / Northumberland Wildlife Trust

Popular with walkers, these woods flank the deep-sided slopes along the River Allen and its tributary valleys.

Dormice, red squirrel, otter, roe deer, badger, mink and stoat are among the animals at home here, together with more than 60 species of bird.

A network of occasionally steep and muddy paths leads through the woodland and beside the river. Try the 4km (2.5mile) route from Allen Banks car park through Victorian ornamental woodland to Plankey Mill – this encompasses the entire site. More adventurous visitors can continue to Staward Gorge, a more rugged area to the south, to look for the ruins of a medieval peel tower and gatehouse.

Woodlands here are largely ancient with oak and wych elm growing above a rich ground flora including mochatel, while 18th century beech and conifers prevail elsewhere. One of the joys of this site is encountering the meadow where wild pansies grow adjacent to a stand of conifers at Allen Banks.

MAP 1

Letah Wood

Letah Wood

Hexham

Taking B6306 from Hexham,
turn right signed Newbiggin.
In Newbiggin turn right into Hill
Road, the main entrance to the
wood and car park is on the left.
(NY939604)
14 ha (35 acres)
The Woodland Trust

See Letah Wood in early spring
and you'll be greeted by the
rare and wonderful sight of
wild daffodils − a clue to its
ancient origins. And whenever
you visit you'll hear the
bubbling sounds of Letah Burn
as it tumbles by.

Thought to be
Northumberland's last wild
daffodil wood, Letah has
witnessed their numbers
increasing over recent decades.

Once part of the Newbiggin
Estate, which dates back to the
14th century, woods have
existed here for centuries. The
original cover of oak, ash and
elm was supplemented with
non-native trees such as beech
and conifers and, since the
19th century, the wood has

been a mixture of broadleaves and conifers. Seek out, in particular, the massive specimens of beech and Douglas fir.

Red squirrels share the wood with roe deer, fox and stoat and a bird population that includes jay, wagtail, hawfinch, redwing and blackcap.

Juliets Wood
Hexham

From A695 east of Hexham, take B6307 to Slaley/Blanchland. Turn left at T-junction with B6036 and left again into Slaley village and park on left near bungalows. Follow footpath north to Marley Cote Walls and the wood is reached after approx 1km (0.75mile). (NY977587)
8 ha (20 acres)
Northumberland Wildlife Trust

A good half-mile walk across open fields set in beautiful rolling countryside leads you here.

Juliets Wood consists of two areas of ancient woodland, separated by a more recently planted area. Predominately oak, with sparse hazel coppice and patchy holly beneath, remnant ancient woodland species such as moschatel and wood anemone, wood speedwell, woodrush and ferns emerge from the woodland floor.

Birdlife includes barn, tawny and little owls, wood warbler, pied flycatcher and tree creeper. Mammals occasionally glimpsed include stoat, weasel and roe deer.

The site has a welcoming, open feel to it, with a discrete waymarked path through the centre that is generally easy for walking. A quiet, 'off the beaten track' wood in which to enjoy a gentle stroll.

MAP 1

Nunsbrough Wood
Ordley

Follow B6306 south of Hexham, turning right for Newbiggin and then follow signs for Ordley. There are three public entrances to the wood: main entrance is from Ordley village, another is from the south on the public footpath that leads through the wood and a further one from the north across Linnelswood Bridge. (NY950595) 16 ha (40 acres)

The Woodland Trust

The twists and turns of Devil's Water, south of Hexham, add drama to Nunsbrough Wood which lines the steep slopes of the gorge.

Although secluded, the woodland is served by a waymarked public footpath running north to south. A permissive path leads down to the large riverside meadow where summer grazing encourages many flowers including the scented meadowsweet, lady's smock and lady's mantle.

Nunsbrough Wood

The flow in this section of the Devil's Water is highly active. The resulting bank-side erosion creates a natural yet rare habitat.

The woodland itself is dominated by mature oak and ash planted in the 1920s, with two recently planted areas north and south of the meadows.

Small clusters of alder line the more fertile, wet ground at the base of the slopes alongside sycamore, lime, horse chestnut and elm. A variety of ferns and flora provide attractive ground cover including dog's mercury, yarrow, pignut, wood-sorrel and germander speedwell.

Slaley
Colpitts Grange

In centre of Hexham take B6306 signed Slaley. Carry on past Slaley village. Car park on right just after entering forest. (NY978552)
511 ha (1263 acres)
Forestry Commission

Entering Slaley is a little like stepping through the back of the wardrobe and into the wild, windswept forest of Narnia.

Part of a big, bold landscape, this is a dark and tangled plantation, where bracing winds whistle through the trees and the smell of conifers is heady.

Despite being close to the beautiful market town of Hexham and its role as a working forest, Slaley has a remote feel, with huge, austere and often dense conifers – a wonderful place to get away from it all.

Interestingly, the forest is occasionally used for husky racing and training.

Wander the forest tracks for a real sense of the great outdoors where woodland scenery changes and surprises await. This is a great place for children to exercise both their bodies and imaginations beneath conifers, knee deep in heather. The more adventurous can continue through the forest and onto Blanchland Moor.

MAP 1

Pontburn Woods
Hamsterley Mill

Take A692 from A1 and follow south toward Consett. At Burnopfield take the B6310 towards Hamsterley Mill. A small car park is located off this road on the right just before the bridge over the Pont Burn at Hamsterley Mill. Access to the woods is available across the road from the car park. (NZ145551) 22 ha (54 acres)

The Woodland Trust

Important features on the Derwent Valley landscape, Pontburn Woods are popular with local people, who enjoy good access via a comprehensive path network.

Dissected by the Derwent Walk, the site is actually a mosaic of conifer high forest and broadleaves, including ancient woodland, and represents one of the valley's largest remaining areas of deciduous woodland.

Nuthatches number among a healthy population of breeding birds which thrive, along with many rare insects, including the

Pontburn Woods

brown lacewing.

Most of the woodland grows on the slopes straddling Pont Burn, one of a number of watercourses that flow through the woods. Alder grows in the wetter areas, whilst drier slopes consist largely of oak and birch. The main area of deciduous woodland is dominated by oak, ash and elm.

The shrub layer includes holly, hawthorn, rowan, elder and hazel and, come spring, wood-sorrel, bluebell and wood anemone add their colour.

Chopwell Woodland Park
High Spen

From A1 take A694 south. After Rowlands Gill take B6315 right towards High Spen. Wood is a couple of miles on the left. (NZ139589)
375 ha (927 acres)
Forestry Commission

Walkers, cyclists and riders from nearby Tyne and Wear enjoy the many facilities provided at Chopwell Woodland Park.

A conifer plantation with mixed deciduous woodland in places, it offers solitude and tranquillity as well as exercise, yet human activity doesn't prevent the park from bristling with wildlife. It supports more than 250 plant species, 95 different types of bird and a variety of mammals including red squirrel and roe deer.

The forest has a long history of fuelling the North East's ship building, coal-mining and bridge-building industries and remains a working wood with pine, larch and fir still felled for their timber. The remains of a mineral railway feature on one of the woodland walks.

A range of waymarked trails offer good access through this well-managed forest, where creative sculptures add extra interest. A highlight of the programme is the not-to-be-missed Chopwell Forest Festival – a popular event each July that attracts thousands of visitors.

MAP 1

Whittle Dene
Ovingham

Ovingham lies just south of the
A69. Park in the village and follow
the public footpath which passes
beside mill buildings and heads
northwest. The path enters the
wood at its southern boundary.
(NZ072656)
20 ha (49 acres)
The Woodland Trust

Set in a countryside haven,
Whittle Dene is one of the
first stretches of wooded land
you come across when
travelling west of Newcastle.

Wildlife thrives in this
secluded piece of ancient
woodland. The range of plant
and insect life here has
benefitted from coppicing,
which allows more light to
reach the woodland floor and
thereby encourages flowers.

As a result, the site is home
to all sorts of wildlife ranging
from breeding sparrowhawks
to red squirrels, deer and, it is
believed, even otters. Bats and
birdlife – including willow
warbler, kestrel and owl – help
bring the woods to life.

Whittle Dene has an
industrial past. At the southern
end of the wood are the
remains of a mill pond, a well,
weir structures and derelict
buildings – all that's left of a
water-driven flourmill. The
millpond has since been
colonised by willow and alder.

Gibside
Rowlands Gill

Entrance on B6314 between
Burnopfield and Rowlands Gill.
From A1 take exit north of Metro
Centre and follow brown tourism
signs. (NZ172583)
163 ha (403 acres) SSSI

The National Trust

One of the North East's finest
examples of 18th century
landscapes, Gibside in the
Derwent Valley is a beautiful
park and pleasure ground –
and just a stone's throw from
Gateshead and Newcastle.

This is a park for people. It
provides a spectacular
backcloth for a year-round
programme of events and the
visitors who flock to take part
are well served with

information, shopping and
refreshment facilities and
a landscape with a real
'genteel' feeling.

There is a pacey mixture of
deciduous woodland, dense
conifer plantations and
columns of exotic parkland
trees. The Gibside Tree Trail
details the changing landscapes
at Gibside through the ages.
Four waymarked walks range
from short strolls hugging the
car park to more challenging
hikes up towards the Column
of Liberty, one of a host of
features standing out among
the trees.

Other highlights include the
Palladian Chapel and Long
Walk, the Walled Garden,
Banqueting House and the
ruins of Gibside Hall.

Gibside

MAP 1

Thornley Wood, Derwent Walk Country Park
Rowlands Gill

From A1 take A694 south towards
Rowlands Gill. Pass The Golden
Lion pub on left and follow road
until visitor centre sign for
Thornley Woodland Centre on
left. (NZ178603)
60 ha (150 acres) SSSI
Gateshead Council

A short journey is all that is
needed to whisk you away
from the urban buzz of
Gateshead or Newcastle to the
pristine beauty of one of the
North East's most outstanding
ancient woodlands.

With a long history as a
working wood, the woodland
of the Derwent Walk Country
Park is populated by oaks, ash
and hazel coppice and at its
colourful best in spring, with a
riot of bluebells, lesser
celandine and ramsons.

A perfect complement to a
stroll through the woods is
neighbouring Derwenthaugh
Park, a former cokeworks
planted recently with thousands
of trees. Fully accessible to
walkers and cyclists alike, it
provides the perfect entrance
to the woodland via the
Derwent Walk.

The Country Park boast two
observation hides, perfect for
the dawn chorus, and a
meander down by the river
provides a chance to spot an
otter. A full events programme
is available from the
information centre.

Watergate Forest Park & Washingwell Woods
Gateshead

Follow signs off A1 to Lobley Hill
and A692. Car park (offering
wheelchair access) at top of
Lobley Hill on Whickham Highway
(B6317) beside Gateshead Central
Nursery. Small car park beside
Emmanuel College on A692.
(NZ222598)

Gateshead Council

Following the demise of the
coal-mining industry, the
landscape at Watergate Forest
Park was given a new lease
of life – a great example of
how post-industrial areas
can recover.

Within easy reach of Newcastle and Gateshead, this is a place to relish with lots of space, wildlife, pathways, sculptures and views across the landscape to the dramatic *Angel of the North*.

Watergate Colliery, on the outskirts of Gateshead, was transformed following reclamation work in the 1990s. Attractions in the revitalised park include an arboretum, national willow collection and what are called the Green Heart and Floating Rock sculptures.

A series of trails and paths, with routes from one to three miles long, leads through new and existing woodland, around a lake and by heather moorland and wildflower meadows.

Washingwell Wood, known locally as the bluebell wood, is just a short walk way. Mainly coniferous woodland, it once provided pit-props for the colliery.

Carrickshill Wood
Stanley

Take A6076 south from Gateshead towards Stanley. Opposite right turn to Causey Arch, turn left by pub/hotel into Beamishburn Road. Take first minor road on left at small white cottage. Car park signed Beamish Burn picnic site, 200m on right. (NZ204546)
10 ha (25 acres)
Durham County Council

Just a few miles from the centre of bustling Gateshead, Carrickshill Wood is a delightful woodland.

Great for families, it has a picnic area, space to play and a beautiful stream. But the main attraction are the trees which range from 40-year-old conifer plantations to distinctive oaks, ashes and willows that date back 200 or 300 years. At the heart of the Great North Forest, Carrickshill is wonderful in spring with its white carpet of ramsons.

A descriptive walk leads through the woods as part of the Tyne and Wear Trail with interpretation boards describing different tree species along the way.

With the Beamish Museum just 1km away, why not combine a visit with Carrickshill for a fun day out.

Hedley Hall

Hedley Hall
Sunniside

From Stanley follow A6076 north. After passing Causey station on left take next turning right. Car park on right. (NZ218559)
43 ha (107 acres) SSSI
The Woodland Trust

Visitors flock to Hedley Hall Woods, a flagship site in the Great North Forest and a favourite for informal recreation and community events.

The woods occupy a tranquil setting close to Beamish Museum and are made up of Ridley Gill, a 9ha (22 acre) SSSI ancient woodland and a 46ha (115 acre) woodland creation scheme where broadleaved trees and shrubs have been planted on former arable and pasture land.

Running along the western edge, you can see the varied canopy of Ridley Gill rising out of the valley. Here are three distinct high forest woodland types – oak, the regionally uncommon wet alder and ash–elm woodland. Tussock sedge grows in abundance in the wet alder woodland.

Set on gently undulating land, Hedley Hall includes a large hay and wild flower meadow, a peat bog and a large glade where visitors can relax. Look for sculpted wooden seats and artwork along the Sculpture Trail which runs through the site.

Hell Hole Wood
Beamish

Follow signs for Beamish Open Air Museum. As you leave the A693 at the roundabout heading towards the museum entrance, parking is available on the left. From the corner of the car park a track leads eastwards towards the wood. (NZ209540)
19 ha (48 acres)
The Woodland Trust

Local people love to relax and play in Hell Hole Wood, a popular site within the Great North Forest.

However it is the red squirrel that may help to shape the future of this ancient woodland site close to Beamish in County Durham. A survey indicates that large numbers think this is not such a Hell Hole.

This has caused the Woodland Trust to re-think plans to fell the Japanese larch, Corsican pine, Scots pine and Douglas fir that dominate the site today, as part of a programme to restore its native broadleaves.

A Sustrans cycleway runs along the southern boundary of this wood, which is well used by local people. Access to the wood is by a good network of permissive footpaths and a public footpath through the northwest section. The main path leads you into adjoining Carrickshill Wood (see page 45).

Three small burns run through the wood, chief of them being Letch Burn which flows through a steep sided gully.

Hell Hole Wood

MAP 2

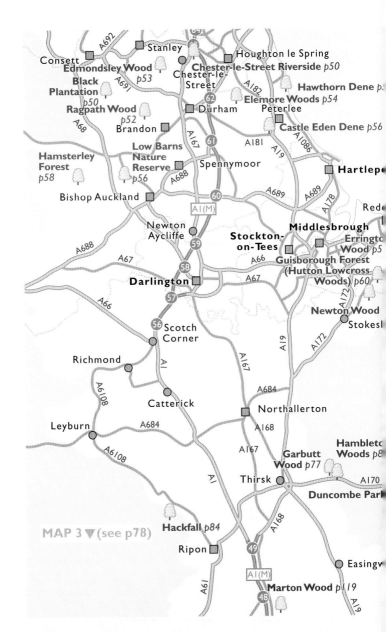

Consett

Stanley

Houghton le Spring

Edmondsley Wood *p53*
Black Plantation *p50*

Ragpath Wood *p52*

Brandon

Chester-le-Street Riverside *p50*

Chester-le-Street

Hawthorn Dene *p.*

Elemore Woods *p54*

Peterlee

Durham

Castle Eden Dene *p56*

Hamsterley Forest *p58*

Low Barns Nature Reserve *p56*

Spennymoor

Hartlepo

Bishop Auckland

Newton Aycliffe

Red

Stockton-on-Tees

Middlesbrough

Errington Wood *p5*

Guisborough Forest (Hutton Lowcross Woods) *p60*

Darlington

Newton Wood

Stokesl

Scotch Corner

Richmond

Catterick

Northallerton

Leyburn

Hamblet Woods *p8*

Garbutt Wood *p77*

Thirsk

Duncombe Parl

MAP 3 ▼(see p78)

Hackfall *p84*

Ripon

Easingv

Marton Wood *p119*

48

MAP 1 ▲ (see p16)

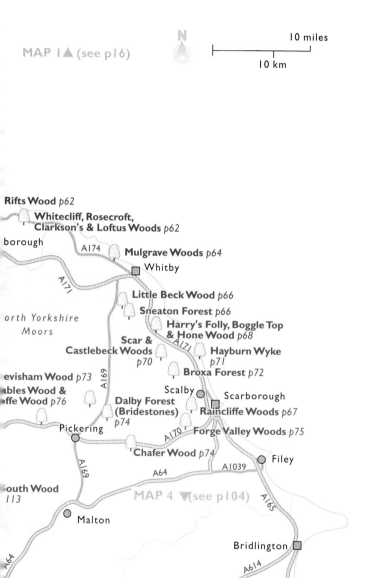

N

10 miles

10 km

Rifts Wood *p62*

Whitecliff, Rosecroft, Clarkson's & Loftus Woods *p62*

borough

A174   Mulgrave Woods *p64*

Whitby

A171

Little Beck Wood *p66*

Sneaton Forest *p66*

orth Yorkshire Moors

Harry's Folly, Boggle Top & Hone Wood *p68*

Scar & Castlebeck Woods *p70*

A171   Hayburn Wyke *p71*

Broxa Forest *p72*

evisham Wood *p73*

A169

Scalby

Scarborough

bles Wood & ffe Wood *p76*

Dalby Forest (Bridestones) *p74*

Raincliffe Woods *p67*

Pickering

A170   Forge Valley Woods *p75*

Chafer Wood *p74*

A169

A64

A1039   Filey

outh Wood *113*

MAP 4 ▼ (see p104)

A165

Malton

A64

Bridlington

A614

MAP 2

Chester-le-Street Riverside
Chester-le-Street

Leaving the A1 at Chester-le-Street junction, take the A167 south heading towards Durham. At the first roundabout turn left, you will see the cricket ground on the right. At the next minor roundabout, turn left into Riverside car park. (NZ282510)
50 ha (124 acres)
Chester-le-Street District Council

For a dramatic entry to the countryside try Chester-le-Street Riverside.

Few other North East sites offer the same mix of historic woodland, architectural features, modern change, artistic adventure and riverside babble.

Here, in the heart of town, are ornamental gardens, picnic areas and riverside walks in beautiful countryside overlooked by Lumley Castle. It has all you need for a group stroll or long distance adventure – and as part of the Great North Forest there is a huge range of recreational opportunities.

The River Wear, with its thriving birdlife, riverside trail and large nature area has great places to rest and observe.

On the opposite bank, a public right of way runs through the woodland of the Scarborough Estate, where a good mix of deciduous species surround the castle. Access can be difficult, particularly in winter, but the spring flora is worth the effort.

Black Plantation
Lanchester

Take B6296 southwest of Lanchester following signs for Satley. Once over river bridge, wood is on left. Parking for one to two vehicles is available in the lay-by just before the wood. (NZ136449)
14 ha (34 acres)
The Woodland Trust

Lying on the south bank of the River Browney, near Lanchester village, Black Plantation is a site packed with variety and interest.

Roe deer, foxes, various birds and the uncommon orange underwing moth are among

Black Plantation

the many wildlife species to be found here.

Dominated by birch with the occasional oak, beech, willow and Scots pine the site was enriched with an oak planting programme in 2001. An opportunity for visitors to see tomorrow's wood in the making.

The western half of the site is wet birch woodland with grasses and ferns beneath. On the east it is much drier, dominated by birch with some oak and beech. Here you will find a good mix of holly, hazel, guelder rose and bird cherry. Ground cover includes wild strawberry, lesser celandine, dog violet, wood-sorrel and common bugle.

A circular route leads through the wood via a network of permissive paths.

MAP 2

Ragpath Wood
Esh Winning

Take B6302 west from Durham to
Esh Winning. Park in the village,
walk along Station View then turn
left to follow the minor road
round onto Woodland Terrace.
At the end of Woodland Terrace a
bridleway leads into the wood.
(NZ199418)
33 ha (82 acres)
The Woodland Trust

Ragpath Wood is a large mixed
woodland set in the Deerness
Valley. Spread across the steep
hillside overlooking the old
mining village of Esh Winning,
Ragpath forms the eastern end
of a plantation belt covering
the valley's southern side.

The wood is an ancient
woodland site planted in the
1950s with larch, Scots pine,
spruce, sycamore and beech,
though a scattering of oak and
birch still survives.

It is popular, not just with
locals but also large numbers
from outside the valley since
the old railway line sandwiched
between the wood and village

Ragpath Wood

now forms part of the Deerness Valley Walk.

While the sparse understorey is dominated by holly, many of the steep slopes have a layer of heather, bilberry, gorse and broom. Head for the flatter areas by the river to enjoy carpets of ramsons, wood anemone and wood-sorrel. Look too for insectivorous butterbur plants.

Edmondsley Wood
Chester-le-Street

From A167 head for Waldridge Fell and then on to Edmondsley village. Go straight over crossroads and park 300m on right after the allotments. (NZ228494)
13 ha (32 acres)
Durham Wildlife Trust

Despite the slightly off-putting entrance this wood proves to be a jewel the further you explore into it.

A mixture of ancient woodland, wetlands and open marsh areas, you'll be rewarded with the site of fine veteran trees, especially birch and oak, with their wonderfully twisted, gnarled forms.

A sense of peacefulness pervades this well-cared-for wood where coppiced hazel material is being used to protect young trees, and path improvement is taking place. Despite this, some footpaths remain a challenge.

MAP 2

Elemore Woods

Elemore Woods

Easington Lane

Follow Elemore Lane southwest
out of Easington Lane towards
High Pittington. Park in the hamlet
of Elemore Vale and walk past the
public house southwards and
follow the public footpath across
the fields to the wood.
(NZ355440)
70 ha (174 acres)

The Woodland Trust

Set in the heart of a stretch of
arable farmland, Elemore
Woods is a wildlife haven set
on the magnesian limestone
plateau that lies southwest
of Easington Lane in
County Durham.

This conifer-dominated site is
dotted with occasional
broadleaves – sycamore, ash,
beech and elm – which used to
abound before the site was
replanted in the early 1960s.
Wych elm is common,
particularly among the
understorey.

The beech areas, in particular,
are worth visiting in the
autumn when their leaves take
on wonderfully vibrant hues.

The shrub layer is well developed in some parts, with hazel and holly forming dense thickets and providing an important food source for small mammals such as wood mice. Robins, woodpeckers and wrens may be seen year-round. In early summer, the ground flora of dog's mercury, red campion and columbine, is alive with humming bees.

An extensive network of footpaths and tracks weaves through the site.

Hawthorn Dene
Seaham

Leave A19 at Easington on B1283. Turn left onto B1432 to Hawthorne village. Take first right after village. Park at cottage. (NZ433457)
69 ha (170 acres) SSSI
Durham Wildlife Trust

Durham's second largest coastal dene is Hawthorn Dene, a relatively unspoilt woodland clothing the steep sides of a magnesian limestone ravine.

Ash, elm and sycamore trees dominate the woodland and mature yews stand out on the steep northern slopes while the woodland floor is carpeted with a colourful spring display of wild garlic, bluebell and snowdrop. Less common species such as early purple orchid, bird's nest orchid and herb paris also grow here.

Alert visitors might be lucky to spot a roe deer, fox or badger and the bird population includes jay, tree creeper, green and great spotted woodpeckers.

Over in the eastern part of the reserve there is an area of grassland where summer visitors – particularly those coming in July and August – can enjoy vast numbers of butterflies drawn by the abundance of ground flora including fairy flax, quaking grass, bloody cranesbill and dyers greenwood.

MAP 2

Castle Eden Dene
Castle Eden

Follow brown tourist signs on A19 and from Peterlee. Car park off Durham Way. (NZ410387)

222 ha (549 acres)

English Nature

'A truly breathtaking journey' – one visitor's description of a walk through the award-winning Castle Eden Dene National Nature Reserve. Set on the northern edge of The Tees Forest, this wildlife haven forms the North East's largest area of woodland.

The 6.5km (4 miles) expanse of wild ancient woodland runs along a deep, steep gorge where mystic yews emerge from strange rocks, and which for thousands of years has spawned stories, poetry and tales of the Devil.

Exploration is via a 12-mile network of paths and more than 25 footbridges, though sturdy footwear is needed on steep, sometimes slippery routes. An eight-mile round trip takes visitors through a tangled network of yews, oaks, ash and dying elms before the crash of waves heralds their arrival at the vast Durham coastline.

The dene features a wealth of wildflowers, 300 different fungi and, with more than 3,000 species, is one of the North East's richest insect habitats. In winter you might spot red squirrels or hear tawny owls at night. Less common sights are the roe deer, foxes and badgers.

Low Barns Nature Reserve
Witton-le-Wear

Take minor road off A68 through village of Witton-le-Wear. Look for brown tourist sign. (NZ163313)

50 ha (124 acres) SSSI

Durham Wildlife Trust

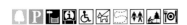

Born out of a former gravel pit, this young woodland of spruce, larch, pine, oak and rowan, willow, poplar and alder surrounds an attractive lake.

A well-surfaced path around the lake gives access to three bird hides, a dipping platform, and bird feeding station. Other habitats include a butterfly garden, grazed grassland, shallow pools and wet flushes where alder is being coppiced.

The site has a pleasant, open aspect and provides easy access for all.

Errington Wood
New Marske

From A174 head south to New Marske and Grewgrass Lane, turn left at the top of the hill into picnic area. (NZ618203)
80 ha (198 acres)
Langbaugh on Tees Borough Council

At the heart of The Tees Forest, Errington Wood has attracted Man since the Stone Age.

A circular walk around the wood offers the chance to enjoy sights, sounds and history – and drink in the contrasting Teesside scenery from the imposing coastline at Saltburn across to Guisborough and the moors.

Bronze Age chieftains were buried here. Later it became a centre for ironstone mining. The wood has been forested for more than 100 years and is popular today with walkers. Work is underway to enrich its habitats by supplementing the dominant pine, larch and spruce with oak, ash, birch, cherry and beech.

An open grassland area, dotted with gorse, elder, rose and thorn, teems with insect and birdlife. Some 90 bird species have been recorded, along with hedgehogs, stoats, roe deer, foxes and badgers.

A good network of paths serves the site, which can be enjoyed as part of the Upleatham Hills circular walk.

MAP 2

Hamsterley Forest
Bishop Aukland

Follow A689 towards Wolsingham. On nearing Wolsingham turn right towards Chatterley. Continue along minor road (Shull Bank) and turn right just before Bedburn into Redford Lane. Take first left, car park 250m on right. (NZ092313)

2500 ha (6179 acres) SSSI

Forestry Commission

County Durham's largest forest, Hamsterley is also one of its most popular tourist attractions.

There is little surprise at its appeal. Hanging on the edge of the North Pennines Area of Outstanding Natural Beauty, between the Durham Dales and Teesdale, its peace and creativity is a natural wonder in its own right.

More than 150,000 visitors arrive every year and yet the tranquillity of this special place is to be savoured. The serenity of walking alongside Low Redford Meadow, a Site of Special Scientific Interest with more than 100 species of plants, surrounded by a vast array of birdlife including pied flycatchers, woodpeckers and nightjars is a wonderfully calming experience.

This working forest centres on the steep valley of the Ayhope and Bedburn becks and houses a rich and varied collection of habitats. Conifer covers much of the site with some mature Scots pine more than 70 years old. Along Bedburn Beck are areas of mixed and broadleaved woodland including 62 acres of oak woods.

Hamsterley is brimming with wildlife – no wonder acclaimed naturalist David Bellamy made his home nearby! Roe deer and badgers feature among an array of mammals that thrive on this site. The forest is also renowned for its large population of reptiles and collection of butterflies.

A real treat is the tree walk, where you can find some of the oldest specimens in the forest. Planted last century by the Surtees family, mature monkey puzzle, giant redwood and yew stand today alongside a variety of creative sculptures.

A 6.5km (4 miles) forest drive provides access to six waymarked trails and picnic areas so it is easy to explore widely – if you have the time. Those who prefer a brisker pace can take advantage of the full events programme or call at the visitor centre and pick up details of the many walking, cycling, horse riding and orienteering opportunities Hamsterley affords.

MAP 2

Guisborough Forest (Hutton Lowcross Woods)

Guisborough

A171 east from Middlesbrough, after 4 km (2.5 miles) on dual carriageway take the A173. Car park is 800m on left after minor road to Guisborough. (NZ585152) 478 ha (1181 acres)

Forestry Commission

Guisborough Forest, gateway to the North York Moors National Park and The Tees Forest, extends a warm welcome to visitors, with excellent access and enviable views over Guisborough and nearby Roseberry Topping.

This prominent local landscape feature is a mixed commercial woodland dominated by Corsican and Scots pine, spruce and larch with pockets of cherry, ash, sycamore and beech.

The Cleveland Way passes through the forest, which is well served with a visitor centre, tracks, bridleways, footpaths, orienteering and mountain bike courses, and provides a full programme of events. If you want to explore further, take a circular walk to the Topping but wear strong boots.

Bold Venture Gill is a regionally important geological site within the forest where the landscape is punctured with rocky outcrops and airshafts from former ironstone mines.

Listen out for the haunting call of a curlew or lapwing, increasing in numbers here. Or you might spot other ground-nesting birds such as snipe or golden plover.

Newton Wood
Newton under Roseberry

Following the A173 turning right
into Roseberry Lane near Newton
under Roseberry. At the end of
this road turn right into Newton
Wood. (NZ575126)
8 ha (20 acres) SSSI
The National Trust

Sandwiched between the
uniquely shaped landmark
Roseberry Topping and the
village of Newton-under-
Roseberry, is Newton Wood, a
year-round canvas of subtly
changing greens and browns.

This important broadleaved
woodland forms an important
piece in a jigsaw of woods,
moors, town, countryside
and industry. The area is rich
in wildlife, particularly
moorland birds.

Several paths crisscross the
wood, which is mainly mature
oak with higher pockets of ash
and a developing holly
understorey. In the southern
corner of the wood is Cliff Rigg
Quarry where the sheer face
and shale deposits of former
workings are gradually being
covered in gorse and birch.

Most visitors use the internal
paths to create a circular walk
through the wood though it is
possible to create a linear walk
taking in Roseberry Topping
and Guisborough or Easby
Moor. The Topping summit
provides magnificent 360-
degree views reaching – on a
clear day – across The Tees
Forest to Teesside and to the
Yorkshire Dales.

MAP 2

Rifts Wood
Saltburn

Eastern edge of Saltburn Park at pay and display, signposted Beach, Valley Gardens. Follow path along beck though gardens. (NZ666208)
35 ha (87 acres)
Redcar and Cleveland Council

Just minutes from the beach and approached via award-winning Italian gardens complete with miniature railway, Rifts Wood is perfect for restless youngsters.

In spring you'll catch the distinctive aroma of wild garlic. Growing beneath stately oak, ash and beech on the valley sides are hazel, holly and ivy and lower still hart's tongue and broad buckler ferns bask in the moist atmosphere.

Skelton Beck rushes between ironstone outcrops creating microclimates that draw dippers, grey wagtails and even kingfishers. Across the gorge, the neo-Gothic splendour of Rushpool Hall can be glimpsed through the trees.

An elegantly proportioned brick viaduct provides a surprising yet impressive feature and further on are small falls which are particularly spectacular after rain.

Whitecliff, Rosecroft, Clarkson's & Loftus Woods
Loftus

Woods can be accessed from A174 and B1366 south of Loftus. (NZ712184)
23 ha (57 acres)
Redcar and Cleveland Council

Providing a backdrop to the village of Loftus, the woods are an important link with the wildwood. Their survival is due to their steep-sided valley location, since vast upland areas were cleared for crops or minerals. There is ample evidence of the ironstone mining that thrived at nearby Skinningrove and Liverton.

For a great woodland vista, the viaduct near the northwestern edge of Clarkson's Wood provides magnificent valley views with the woods disappearing into the horizon and Kilton Beck escaping to the North Sea.

A maze of paths, footbridges, steps and gullies run through the site.

Mulgrave Woods (see next page)

MAP 2

Mulgrave Woods

Sandsend

A174 east to Sandsend. Lythe Bank continues into Sandsend Road and wood is on right. (NZ861125)

810 ha (2002 acres)

Marquis of Normanby

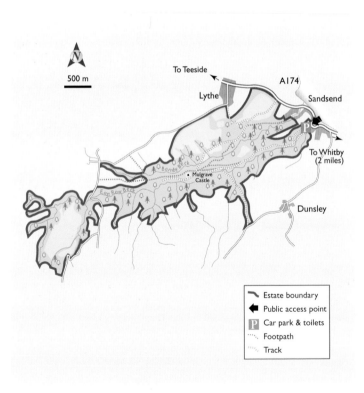

Layers of history, myth and legend combine in Mulgrave Woods – a place of year-round magical fantasy.

Even at 2,000 acres, the woodland is an intimate mix of hardwoods – primarily beech, ash, oak and sycamore – and a softwood cocktail of larch, spruce and fir. Cloaking the sides of two valleys, you'll find outlying native oak woods, alder groves mirroring the river's course and a scattering of exotic specimens which add romance.

Mulgrave is a place to be enjoyed at any time of year from the spring carpets of snowdrops, bluebells and primroses to the colours of autumn and frosty snowscapes that add a dramatic edge later in the year.

As the landscape climbs from sea level to 260 metres (850 ft) areas of open ground allow views both within the wood and vistas that open up across the distant valley, to Whitby Abbey and out to sea.

Step back in time and discover a Victorian wild garden, an arboretum, traces of a carriage path network and two castles. The most ancient of these survives as a motte in the northwest corner of the wood and although it is hidden from view, it is accessible from a public footpath.

The keep of a Norman castle has been carefully preserved, retaining the alterations suggested by the landscape gardener Humphry Repton in 1792. Repton was responsible for many of the features of the woods including a dry arch, stone bridges and the rock tunnel.

The Georgian country house with turrets and battlements added in the early 19th century completes the fantasy.

A continuing programme of selective felling and planting is restoring Repton's vision for the site. Indeed the bulk of the forestry work today involves maintaining and enhancing these landscape features, with the aim of growing quality hardwood crops for the future.

MAP 2

Little Beck Wood
Sneaton

8km (5 miles) west of Robin Hood's Bay. Take B1416 to Littlebeck and park in village hall car park. Reserve entrance 100m down hill by ford. (NZ880050) 13 ha (32 acres)
Yorkshire Wildlife Trust

A tour of this sheltered woodland gem, near the picturesque hamlet of Littlebeck throws up many clues and insights into its past, including a strong industrial heritage and links with the wildwood.

Nestling in a deeply cut valley, the wood has a humid atmosphere allowing fungi and bryophyte communities to thrive. Alders overhang streamside communities of moschatel, saxifrage, fleabane and sneezewort while higher up the valley hazel and holly grow beneath oak and ash.

Shales, exposed by fallen trees, provide evidence of the once all-important 18th-century quarrying for alum here. In spring the wood is resplendent with bluebells, primroses and early purple orchid though an out-of-season visit will provide maximum atmosphere.

Little Beck has good links with nearby Sneaton Forest (see next entry).

Sneaton Forest
Whitby

Take A171 north from Scarborough. Turn left onto B1416 to Sneaton. Turn sharp left into Foss Lane (not minor road to Littlebeck) and follow track downhill to Forestry Commission car park. (NZ888036) 1209 ha (2988 acres)
Forestry Commission

The star visitor attraction is the Falling Foss, a 10-metre-high waterfall that stages a particularly spectacular display.

It lies within the old broadleaved woodland that lines steep valleys and makes up the northern section of the forest. All can be explored via generally well-surfaced paths, new footbridges and ironstone steps.

From this focal point, a number of public footpaths

radiate to give access to the surrounding woods.

One of the paths links to Littlebeck via the Hermitage, a folly carved from a huge boulder, and provides fine views across the surrounding moorland.

Other paths lead out onto the moors via the May Beck Picnic Place and into the nearby Newton House plantation, where the woodland cover changes in character. Here beech is dominant, with pockets of larchwood.

Raincliffe Woods
Scarborough

Follow A171 north out of Scarborough. By Yorkshire Coast College turn left into Lady Edith's Drive. Wood is located 1 km (0.75 mile) along the road on the left hand side. (SE995885)
150 ha (371 acres) SSSI

Scarborough Borough Council

Dominated by larch, Corsican pine and beech trees, along with the presence of a sawmill and well-surfaced ride system, provide a clear pointer to its origins as a commercial plantation.

By following the contours of the landscape, the rides overcome the difficulties of the steep ground and provide easy access. Imagination and stamina are required, however, for those who venture away from the rides and tackle small subsidiary paths.

Picnic tables provided within open glades offer excellent vantage points and wonderful views across to Wykeham Forest and into the Derwent Valley.

Raincliffe is a world away from nearby Forge Valley, though the transition to the more diverse and older site, with its abundance of deadwood habitats, is a subtle and interesting one.

MAP 2

Harry's Folly, Boggle Top & Hone Wood
Ravenscar, Fylingdales

Situated approximately 3km
(2 miles) southwest of Robin
Hood's Bay, within the North York
Moors National Park. (NZ935015)
16 ha (39 acres)

The Woodland Trust

Less than two miles from the
coastal town of Robin Hood's
Bay, these adjacent woods form
part of a much larger chain of
ancient woodland.

Relatively undisturbed,
Harry's Folly was extended by
the Woodland Trust in 1998
through a woodland creation
scheme. It is particularly
vibrant during spring and early
summer, thanks to successive
displays of snowdrops,
primroses, bluebells and
daffodils. Dominated by oak
and ash, the wood has a dense
understorey of hazel.

Nearby Boggle Top was
created in 2001 with the
backing of the local
community and planted with
native species including oak,
ash, rowan, field maple and
cherry. Seating provided at the
southern end of the wood
offers magnificent views across
Robin Hood's Bay.

Few outside influences have
touched neighbouring Hone
Wood, a 9.5 acre oak-
dominated ancient woodland
rich in plant species.
Inaccessible for decades, it can
now be reached via Boggle
Top. No paths have been
created, in order to protect the
undisturbed woodland, so
please tread with care.

Harry's Folly

MAP 2

Scar & Castlebeck Woods

Harwood Dale

Follow signs from A171 for Harwood Dale. (SE946971)
52 ha (130 acres) SSSI

The Woodland Trust

If you have ever wanted to tread in the footsteps of dinosaurs, visit Scar & Castlebeck Woods in the beautiful North York Moors National Park.

The secluded woods straddle a steep ravine carved by the streams and small rivers that run off the moors – among them Castlebeck, Jugger How Beck and Bloody Beck, cited as one of the best inland exposures of dinosaur footprints.

Scar & Castlebeck Woods

Designated a Site of Special Scientific Interest, it is home to 23 nationally scarce insects and is the most north-easterly place to find the brimstone butterfly.

Trout, kingfisher and heron abound in the river while the woods are home to many bird species including owl, woodpecker, woodcock and pied flycatcher.

A wealth of mosses and liverworts flourish on the damp valley sides while ferns and grasses thrive on the moderately acidic soils. Scar Wood also boasts some of Britain's largest examples of rare hay-scented buckler fern.

A public footpath provides good access but wellingtons are recommended.

Hayburn Wyke
Scarborough

Take A171 north from Scarborough. Turn right at Cloughton onto minor road signposted Ravenscar. Wood is 2km (1 mile) on right behind Hayburn Wyke Hotel. (TA010970)

The National Trust

This sheltered valley, with its rich mix of moisture-loving plants, including bryophytes, fungi and moschatel, may not be the easiest to find but is well worth it.

One of the most attractive ways to reach the wood is via a circular, 7km (4 mile) walk from Cloughton along a dismantled railway and then returning on a section of the Cleveland Way.

If arriving by road, a footpath from the car park runs left through a yard alongside a barn and into a field. Follow yellow markers until you reach the National Trust sign then either take the path to the cliffs or head northwest down to Hayburn Beck.

Just when you think this steep-sided woodland is a predictable mix of oak and ash, up pops a sweet chestnut. Then larch, spruce and beech put in an appearance on more accessible slopes.

Children will love the stepping stones and following the beck downstream to its outfall, where it rushes over ironstone and to the sea. Here are fine views along the coast.

MAP 2

Broxa Forest
Burniston

At Burniston on the A171 turn west at the sign for Harwood Dale. After 200 metres turn left (for Suffield) and follow the road to the junction at top of the hill 2km (1 mile). Turn right. After 2km (1 mile) the forest lies on either side of the road. (SE965945)
733 ha (1812 acres)
Forestry Commission

From the entertainingly named Turkey Carpet car park, with its veteran oak and boundary trees, you soon enter a contrasting world.

Broxa may be fringed by old broadleaved trees, reminiscent of what the forest would have looked like 50 years ago, but don't be fooled. It's a different story inside. Today's visitor will wander beneath of plantation of larch, Scots pine and some beech.

There are paths that reach the remote sheltered Derwent Valley edged by broadleaved woodland, others that meander past Thieves Dikes and Tumuli and to open areas for fine views across the Cleveland Hills and Roseberry Topping.

For the more energetic, the Allerston Forest Walk strikes west away from the car park to a fine viewpoint before dropping down a steep slope and following the stream to Langdale Bridge. The return via Lowdales Farm along Whisperdales Beck covers a hearty 12 km (7.5 miles).

Levisham Wood
Pickering

Follow A169 north from Pickering for approximately 9km (5.5 miles). Turn left into Lockton village. Follow minor road to Levisham. Turn left at top of village and along to south end of Little Field Lane. Continue along bridleway to enter wood. (SE826896) 64 ha (158 acres)

North York Moors National Park Authority

A visit to Levisham Wood is an opportunity to step back into the golden age of steam.

For steam train is the best mode of transport to approach Newtondale, one of the most spectacular valleys in Yorkshire, where George Stephenson's famous line still echoes to their romantic breath and whistle.

The train provides some of the most spectacular views of the steep-sided valley with its magnificent and rugged scenery, picturesque villages and swathes of woodland, Levisham Wood being part of a wider woodland complex.

Much of the valley's original woodland cover – oak, ash, birch and lime – has survived. The occasional clutch of conifers adds a dash of texture and colour to the bare broadleaf outlines in winter.

It is easy, using the extensive network of paths, to explore remote corners, where splendid valley views can be gained.

Levisham Wood

MAP 2

Dalby Forest (Bridlestones)
Pickering
From Scarborough turn north off A170 at Thorton-le-Dale. After 3km (2 miles) turn right into Forest Drive. (SE857874) 3598 ha (8893 acres)
Forestry Commission

Adorning a landscape shaped by the Ice Age, Dalby Forest is a vast man-made creation that provides the visitor with a memorable experience that is unique in Britain.

The ancient forest now gone, the site on the southern slopes of the North York Moors National Park has evolved into a hugely popular recreational venue and wildlife haven.

But a cruise along the nine mile Dalby Forest Drive – one of a network of excellent forest roads – is a drive down the road of time and a virtual geology field trip through the Jurassic period. Burial mounds, linear earthworks and the remains of a once-flourishing rabbit warren industry dot the forest.

Apart from pockets of deciduous woodland, where primrose and meadowsweet grow, conifers, replanted as a timber resource from the 1920s, dominate the forest. It is home to various birds such as the crossbill, nightjar and harrier, while mammals such as deer and badger also abound.

Chafer Wood
Ebberston
Turn right off A170 from Scarborough, just north of Ebberston village. Wood is 200m up minor road on left. (SE899832) 30 ha (74 acres)
Yorkshire Wildlife Trust

Small is beautiful – as Chafer Wood proves. Dwarfed by nearby Dalby Forest, this is an intimate gem of a wood, intimate and packed with year-round interest.

There is an entrance to the wood near a recently restored walled area known as the Pinfold and King Alfred's Cairn, site of a natural cave that was used as a burial chamber in Neolithic times with its own romantic legend.

A steep climb along a well-surfaced path provides magnificent views across the Vale of Pickering. En route, the wood's character unfolds, the slopes covered with ash, cherry and blackthorn.

Work to clear thorn and bracken is already producing an abundance of lime-loving plants including cowslip, salad burnet and pyramidal orchids. Spring brings carpets of bluebells and wood anemones.

The circular walk descends to the road via Netherby Dale Dykes and returns along the valley bottom with its marsh orchids, marigolds and gypsywort.

Forge Valley Woods
Scarborough
Turn north off the A170 at East Ayton and follow road next to river. Wood is on either side of river. (SE985865)
95 ha (235 acres) SSSI
Scarborough Borough Council

Woods have been present in the Forge Valley for 6,000 years and this tranquil, mixed deciduous woodland where fox, otter and deer thrive today, preserves an ancient link with the wildwood.

The origins of the valley's name date back to the 14th century when charcoal was produced for local forges.

A walk along the Derwent River – where greyling, trout and crayfish thrive – leads through alder groves that give way to ash woodland on the limestone slopes. Higher up the valley oak is more prominent and there is a dense understorey of hazel, holly and thorn.

The rock is exposed in dramatic sheer faces. Petrified springs in Scarwell Wood illustrate the eerie effect of the limestone deposits.

The woodland sustains a variety of birds from grey wagtail and kingfisher to tree creeper and siskin. Flag iris, and primrose add floral interest.

Paths are well surfaced, including some suitable for the less able.

MAP 2

Stables Wood & Roffe Wood
Sinnington

Off the A170 to the west of Pickering. Limited parking available in the village only. (SE748863/SE750862)
8 ha (20 acres)
The Woodland Trust

Stables Wood has had no public access in living memory. However, creation of a neighbouring native broadleaf wood has now opened this up.

Roffe Wood, planted as part of the Trust's millennium 'Woods on your Doorstep' project, is a small community-designed site that is already well used by local people.

A permissive path circling the site continues through Stables Wood, an ancient woodland remnant sitting on a gentle south-facing slope. This provides a reminder of what surrounding agricultural land may once have looked like.

Dominated by oak, the site boasts an especially rich shrub layer brimming with hazel coppice, holly, field maple, dog rose, hawthorn and blackthorn. Undisturbed for years, the rich ground flora is dominated by dog's mercury, bluebells, grasses and mosses.

Stables Wood forms part of a broken chain of woodland that follows the river valley and finally links with the Forestry Commission's vast Cropton Forest.

Duncombe Park
Helmsley

Heading north on A1(M) turn off at J49, onto A168. Turn right onto A170. Take left off this road toward Duncombe Park. Signposted in Helmsley. (SE603832)
165 ha (408 acres) AONB, SSSI
Helmsley Estate

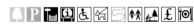

Britain's tallest lime stands proudly in Duncombe Park, a showcase for champion trees.

Overlooking medieval Helmsley Castle and the River Rye Valley, the estate is made up of an impressive early 18th-century house set in 35 acres of landscaped gardens surrounded by 400 acres of parkland. Half is a designated National Nature Reserve and home to scarce wood-eating beetles and the birds that feed on them.

The reserve includes remnants of the wildwood and provides a sanctuary for some of England's oldest and tallest trees.

A well-signed river walk offers fine views across to Helmsley and the moors as the route follows the curve of the river through Terrace Bank Woods.

Although access is restricted to opening hours, the Cleveland Way takes in some of the estate's new coniferous plantations.

Garbutt Wood
Thirlby

Park at Sutton Bank National Park Centre, 9.5km (6 miles) east of Thirsk on A170 to Scarborough, and follow Cleveland Way north. Take the sloping path down the escarpment at the nature trail sign. (SE505835)
24 ha (59 acres) SSSI
Yorkshire Wildlife Trust

There is an air of mystery in Garbutt Wood, where gnarled and twisted veteran oaks and birches lend a 'Tolkeinesque' quality.

This atmospheric site is part of the Sutton Bank National Park Centre and offers a series of rewarding walks through spectacular scenery, including the long-distance Cleveland Way.

Superb views open up almost as soon as you enter and a well-marked nature trail leads through open bracken areas, dotted with birch and mature oak and alive with bluebells in spring. In denser woodland pockets oak, birch, ash, rowan, hazel, holly and hawthorn are supplemented with crab apple, willow and alder that grow by the springs.

It is worth visiting the national park's only natural lake – moody Gormire lake – to catch a glimpse of waterfowl or mini forests of water horsetail.

Heading back towards the Cleveland Way through dew-drenched bilberry and heather, you encounter the sheer face of Whitestone Cliff.

MAP 3

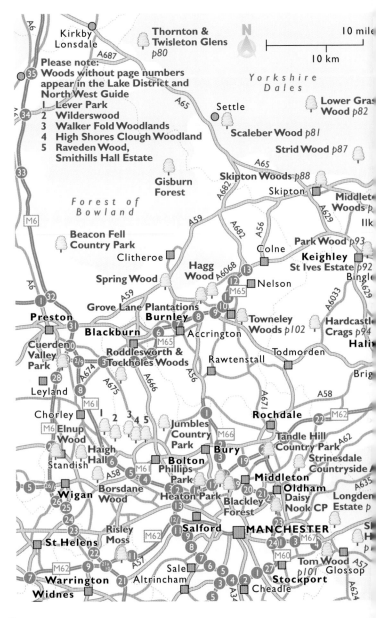

Kirkby
Lonsdale

Thornton &
Twisleton Glens
p80

10 mile

10 km

Please note:
Woods without page numbers
appear in the Lake District and
North West Guide
1 Lever Park
2 Wilderswood
3 Walker Fold Woodlands
4 High Shores Clough Woodland
5 Raveden Wood,
   Smithills Hall Estate

Yorkshire
Dales

Settle

Lower Gras
Wood p82

Scaleber Wood p81

Strid Wood p87

Skipton Woods p88

Skipton

Middlet
Woods p

Ilk

Gisburn
Forest

Forest of
Bowland

Park Wood p93

Keighley
St Ives Estate p92

Bingl

Beacon Fell
Country Park

Clitheroe

Colne

Hagg
Wood

Nelson

Spring Wood

Grove Lane Plantations

Burnley

Towneley
Woods p102

Hardcastl
Crags p94

Hali

Preston

Blackburn

Accrington

Cuerden
Valley
Park

Roddlesworth &
Tockholes Woods

Rawtenstall

Todmorden

Brig

Leyland

Chorley

Elnup
Wood

Haigh
Hall

Standish

Jumbles
Country
Park

A58

A675

A666

A56

A671

A58

Rochdale

M62

Tandle Hill
Country Park

Strinesdale
Countryside

Bolton

Phillips
Park

Bury

Borsdane
Wood

Wigan

Heaton Park

Blackley
Forest

Middleton

Oldham

Daisy
Nook CP

Longden
Estate p

Risley
Moss

Salford

MANCHESTER

St Helens

Sale

Altrincham

Warrington

Widnes

Cheadle

Stockport

Tom Wood
p101

Glossop

S
H
p

78

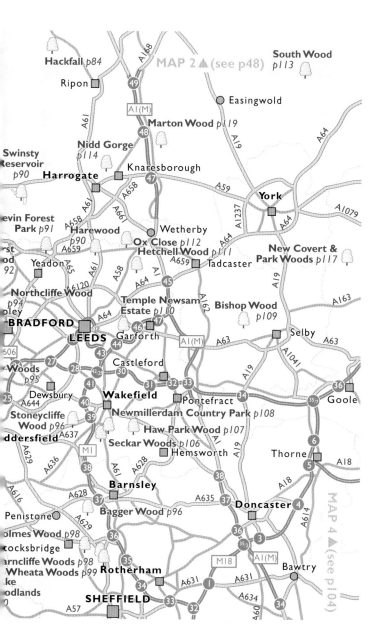

Hackfall *p84*

Ripon

49

MAP 2 ▲ (see p48)

South Wood *p113*

A168

A1(M)

A61

● Easingwold

48

Marton Wood *p119*

A19

A64

Nidd Gorge *p114*

Swinsty Reservoir *p90*

Knaresborough

47

Harrogate

A658

A658

A61

A59

A1237

York

A64

A1079

evin Forest Park *p91*

A658 A61 A661

Harewood *p90*

● Wetherby

Ox Close *p112*

Hetchell Wood *p111*

A659 ■ Tadcaster

A64

A19

New Covert & Park Woods *p117*

rst od *92*

Yeadon

A65

A6120 A61 A658

A58

A64

A1

45

Temple Newsam Estate *p110*

A162

Bishop Wood *p109*

A163

Northcliffe Wood *p94*

pley

BRADFORD

A64

46

47

A1(M)

A63

Selby

A63

LEEDS

Garforth

A1041

606

27

28

43

44

Castleford

A19

36

Woods *p95*

42,25

30

41

31

32 33

34

357

Goole

25

A644

Dewsbury

40

Wakefield

■ Pontefract

Stoneycliffe Wood *p96*

39

Newmillerdam Country Park *p108*

ddersfield A637

Haw Park Wood *p107*

6

A629

A636

M1

Seckar Woods *p106*

A628

■ Hemsworth

A19

Thorne

A18

38

A61

A628

38

A18

Barnsley

A635

5

A616

A636

37

A628

Bagger Wood *p96*

37

Doncaster **4**

A614

Penistone ○

A629

36

A635

36

olmes Wood *p98*

cocksbridge

35.2

3

arncliffe Woods *p98*

Wheata Woods *p99*

ke

35

M18

A1(M)

Bawtry ●

odlands

Rotherham

A631

SHEFFIELD

34

■

A631

1

A631

A634

34

33

A57

32

A60

MAP 4 ▲ (see p104)

MAP 3

Hambleton Woods
Thirlby

A170 east from Thirsk to Sutton
Bank. Wood to east of car park.
(SE515830)
174 ha (430 acres)

Tillhill Forestry

On the eastern edge of the
visitor centre's car park and
across a minor road leading to
Cold Kirby are the remains of
Cleave Dike. Thought to date
from the Bronze Age, this
fragment was once part of an
extensive series of ditches and
banks running north–south for
over 8km (5 miles).

Bisected by the Cleveland
Way, it is thought this follows
the route of the Hambleton
Drove Road, an ancient
highway running from
Scotland to southern England.

The choice of circular walks
and the site's archaeology are its
main draw. Predominantly a
commercial softwood plantation
of spruce, Scots pine and larch,
this is a working wood.

However, there is a long-term
vision for Hambleton which
sees wildlife and landscape
coming more to the fore.

Thornton & Twisleton Glens
Ingleton

On the edge of Ingleton village
parking is provided for the
Waterfalls Walk (signposted) by
the Ingleton Scenery Company.
A charge is made for parking and
access to the woodlands
(SD695750/SD700742)
8 ha (20 acres) SSSI

The Woodland Trust

Ancient woodland is
something of a rarity in
North Yorkshire making
Thornton & Twisleton Glens
all the more valuable.

Situated on the banks of the
River Twiss and River Doe, the
two woods are part of a larger
unbroken chain of ancient
woodland following each
river's course.

Both woods are accessed via
the stunningly beautiful 7km
(4.5 miles) Waterfalls Walk from
Ingleton. Since the late 19th
century, visitors have enjoyed
this route, which combines
ancient oak woodland and
magnificent Dales scenery.

There is a viewing area where you can enjoy a picnic and watch the river fall over limestone rocks in an impressive cascade known as Thornton Force. Also, don't miss Snow Falls beside Twisleton Glen.

Scaleber Wood
Settle

From Settle follow High Hill Lane southeast. A small area for parking directly adjacent to wood. (SD840625)
4 ha (10 acres) SSSI
The Woodland Trust

A real people magnet, Scaleber Wood in the heart of the Yorkshire Dales packs a powerful mix of breathtaking sights and evocative sounds into a small space.

The most spectacular is Scaleber Force, a stunning waterfall whose crystal waters tumble over limestone cliffs before plunging into a deep pool.

The site lies on the Elgar Way – named after the great English composer who was a regular visitor – a 21km (13 mile) circular walk from Settle that takes in impressive crags, gorges and waterfalls.

Scaleber Wood lies within the Attermire Scar, Site of Special Scientific Interest for its remarkable limestone geology with huge outcrops and associated flora.

The wood itself, a mix of broadleaves and planted conifers, may be tricky to access and taxing to explore, but only a short walk from the road is needed to reveal the spectacular sight of the waterfall from a viewpoint.

MAP 3

Lower Grass Wood
Grassington

From Grassington follow Grass Wood Lane north and park where there are a number of lay-bys and a small, Yorkshire Wildlife Trust car park. (SD983651)

8.5 ha (21 acres)

The Woodland Trust

Ancient woodland adorns this stretch of the River Wharfe valley.

The wood has an open character, due to the loss of most elm trees, with a light canopy of sycamore, oak, ash and birch with occasional larch and beech. But Nature is plugging the gaps with dense patches of regenerating hawthorn, birch, beech and ash.

A wealth of colourful flowers includes carpets of bluebells and dog's mercury, orchids during summer and rich carpets of herbs on the steep open riverside slopes. Two 'elling hearths', small stone-lined pits used to produce potash, can be seen here.

Extend your visit by crossing the road to Yorkshire Wildlife Trust's Grass Wood and climb toward open ground at its summit. An extensive programme of restoration work is returning this wood to its former glory.

Lower Grass Wood

Hackfall (see next page)

MAP 3

Hackfall
Grewelthorpe
Follow A6108 north of Ripon. Take first left after North Stainley through Mickley, and right at T-junction to Grewelthorpe. Wood is situated on the edge of Grewelthorpe, on the road towards Masham. Park in Grewelthorpe and walk 200m on road toward Masham, entrance to wood on right. (SE236771)
45 ha (110 acres) AONB, SSSI
The Woodland Trust

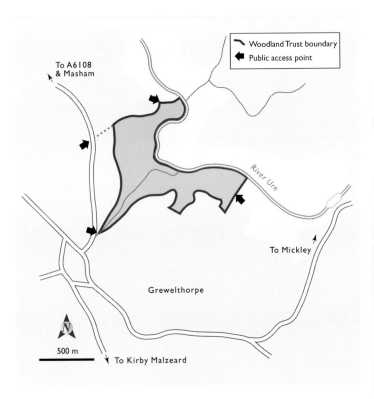

There is something about the wild splendour of Hackfall that simply inspires creativity. Nineteenth-century writers hailed it as one of the most beautiful woodlands in the country while romantic landscape artist Turner painted in it.

Set in a 350ft gorge on the edge of Grewelthorpe, the site was bought in 1731 by John Aislabie, famous for his landscaping work at nearby Fountains Abbey and Studley Royal.

But it was his son, William, who transformed the area into a 'beautiful wilderness', creating grottos and surprise views, glades, rustic temples embedded in groves of trees, waterfalls and follies – many of which can still be discovered in the park today.

In its Victorian heyday, visitors flocked to view the woods and house and to enjoy teas at Mowbray Point, where the Aislabies had entertained friends.

Hackfall

MAP 3

It is possible that conifers were planted in the 19th century to supplement the largely broadleaved woodland but almost the entire wood was felled during the 1930s and regeneration since then has been at the hands of Nature.

For half a century the site fell into decline but since the 1980s, when the Woodland Trust took over, much has been done to return Hackfall to its glory days, restoring footpaths and woodland walks, conserving the various follies, managing the fragile habitats, and giving Hackfall a future.

The ancient woodland is a Site of Special Scientific Interest, along with several other designations. The largely broadleaved area is still dominated by oak with beech, sycamore, ash and even lime originating from the 18th century.

Modern visitors can once again bask in the stunning scenery and enjoy a mass of period features including a host of man-made waterfalls and courses displayed throughout the woodland.

Hackfall teems with wildlife and sustains a thriving range of wild plant communities including a spectacular display of bluebells.

Strid Wood
Bolton Abbey

From A59 turn onto B6160
following signs for Bolton Abbey.
Continue north for approximately
5km (3 miles) to Strid car park on
right. (SE058563)
Sandholme car park entrance
2.5km (1.5 miles) on right from
A59 along B6160. (SE075545)
46 ha (114 acres) SSSI

Trustees of the Chatsworth
Settlement – Yorkshire Estate

Strid Wood has been a popular
destination for almost two
centuries and it is not
surprising, for this is a
woodland for all seasons.

Set along the valley of the
River Wharfe, it forms part of
the Bolton Abbey Estate and
was first opened to visitors in

1810. William Wordsworth
enjoyed the views on frequent
walks through the woods.

The unpolluted waters of the
river gush through the narrow
gorge and support brown
trout, grayling and the
uncommon crayfish while 50
bird species nest in the area. In
summer dragonflies fly over
the water and in winter, ducks
roost on the banks.

Although this is an ancient
woodland site, much of the
valley has been replanted with
beech, sycamore, larch and
spruce. But large areas of sessile
oak provide a valuable habitat
for a variety of wildlife
including rare flowering plants,
fungi and lichens.

Whilst exploring Bolton
Abbey you may like to follow
the Priory Trail to visit
Wandsworth Wood.

MAP 3

Skipton Woods

Skipton Woods
Skipton

From Skipton town centre car park at rear of town hall (pay and display) follow Springs Canal towpath to wood's main entrance. (SD990525)

15 ha (37 acres)

The Woodland Trust

A magical land in the heart of town – that's one way to describe Skipton Woods, a woodland haven by one of Britain's best-preserved, most-popular medieval castles.

The wood's links with the castle date back at least 1,000 years. A canal towpath, following the line of Skipton Castle ramparts and Springs Canal, provides a direct link between the town's High Street and the woods, following the course of Eller Beck through a stunning steep-sided valley.

Most of this ancient woodland is dominated by ash but the occasional sycamore, beech, Scots pine, Norway spruce and hornbeam indicate a greater variety in the past.

The woods are renowned for their vivid displays of bluebells and wild garlic and sustain five species of bat. Green and great spotted woodpeckers add their colour, while kingfisher and heron may be seen fishing the waterways.

In 1998 the Woodland Trust resurfaced paths to allow much easier access.

Middleton Wood
Ilkley

Follow A65 south to Ilkley. Turn into New Brook Street at crossroads in Ilkley and continue up Middleton Avenue and park on roadside on Curly Hill. (SE120488) 45 ha (111 acres)

Bradford Metropolitan Council

Take a walk through Middleton Wood and your surroundings constantly change in character.

These mixed broadleaved amenity woods grow on the terraces created by gritstone outcrops on the hills above Ilkley and feature a stunning display of bluebells each spring.

To the west of the road, areas of sycamore dominate the mix of beech, oak, ash and rowan – a clear contrast with more intimate areas which have narrow winding paths. Elsewhere the understorey of holly creates new character again.

Small streams cascading down the hillside over rocky ledges and mossy boulders are bordered by damp areas where large alders grow in waterlogged soil.

A good network of footpaths links the open country above the wood where you can enjoy wonderful views.

The woodland east of the road is a delightful semi-natural site with much to explore. An abundance of dead timber provides a rich habitat for small birds and insects. There are good paths here too and occasional benches where you can stop to enjoy the woodland scene.

MAP 3

Swinsty Reservoir
Fewston

Take A59 (Skipton Road) east, turn right near Fewston into Cobby Syke Road. Continue to junction near church and turn left to Stack Point car park or turn right and across dam to Swinsty Moor car park. (SE197538)
200 ha (494 acres)
Yorkshire Water

The Washburn Valley reservoirs were built in the 1870's and the surrounding areas planted with a mix of coniferous and broadleaved woodland.

There are a number of circular walks around the reservoirs passing beneath tall Scots pines alongside larch and then through contrasting areas of beech, oak and sycamore.

Views extending across water to the countryside beyond promote a feeling of tranquillity. You can see why local people are attracted back time after time to this peaceful setting.

This is easy and gentle walking country on paths that are well-surfaced and easy to follow, with the water never far away.

Harewood
Harrogate

The village of Harewood is centrally placed in Yorkshire at the junction of the A61/ A659 on the Leeds/Harrogate road. (SE312446)
55 ha (136 acres)
Harewood House Trust

Visitors flock in their thousands to enjoy the sights and sounds of Harewood House and grounds, winner of Yorkshire Tourist Board's 2002 Visitor Attraction of the Year Award.

Open to the public from March to October, the house and grounds include acres of beautiful parkland with trees and mainly broadleaved copses as well as extensive boundary plantations.

Around the lake is a large area of historic amenity woodland, created by Capability Brown, and these areas are managed carefully to preserve the site's landscape heritage.

Visitors can enjoy any number of charming walks through dappled and shaded woods, where the ground is covered in spring bulbs, rhododendron and unusual shrubs.

Chevin Forest Park
Otley

A660 through Otley, following signs to The Chevin. (SE225445) 168 ha (415 acres) SSSI

Leeds City Council

Chevin Forest Park was created for and donated to the residents of Otley as a living memorial to those who gave their lives during World War ll.

Today it is a testament to peace and forms part of the Forest of Leeds where wildlife, including a plethora of birds, lives and thrives.

The woods clothe the steep gritstone escarpment that dominates Otley. Varied and interesting, they include areas of ancient semi–natural woodland with plantations of conifers and mixed broadleaves, including beech, sycamore and oak.

Heather and bilberry grow on the open landscape set above the wood but below the top of the ridge. The green hairstreak butterfly breeds in the gorse scrub while wetter sections support bog asphodel.

There is a good network of walks throughout the area and visitors of all ages and abilities can plan a route that offers variety and attractive scenery. It is possible to walk along the ridge – the reward is magnificent views across every direction.

MAP 3

St Ives Estate
Harden

Follow A650 north near to Bingley.
Turn left onto Harden Road
(B6429). Take right through gate
posts signed St Ives Estate.
Continue up drive to car park
on right. (SE090390)
81 ha (200 acres)

Bradford Metropolitan Council

The St Ives Estate has been
making its mark on English
history for centuries – and
continues to do so.

Once the home of the
crusading monks of the
Knights Hospitallers and
Knights Templar, it is still
contributing to local heritage.
You can see the site of the

Ferrands Oak, a massive 12.5
ton specimen that grew here
for 250 years. It was felled in
1985 and used in the new south
transept of York Minster.

There are other lovely old
trees at St Ives including a
spreading purple beech near
the car park and the remains
of old sweet chestnut further
down the drive.

Once oak and birch
woodland and heather
moorland, the woods have been
replanted with conifers,
broadleaf and mixed woodlands
with rhododendrons and lots of
specimen trees including
wellingtonia, red oak, Bhutan
pine and London plane.

There are several waymarked
walks which can become muddy
so boots are a good idea.

Hirst Wood
Saltaire

Taking A650 south of Bingley, turn
left at roundabout where A657
joins A650 into Clarence Road
(leading to Hirst Lane). Cross
railway line. Car park and wood
on left. (SE132382)
15 ha (37 acres)

Bradford Metropolitan Council

Hirst Wood is something of an
island, separated from
surrounding industrial,
residential and agricultural
landscapes by a perimeter
railway line, river and canal.

Perhaps that is why this
attractive wood is so popular
with local people.

Predominantly oak and
birch, it also has areas of
planted beech that add a

further dimension to your walk as it rises out of the valley of the River Aire. In the southwest corner of the wood the land slopes steeply down to the fast-flowing river – so take special care.

Holly is plentiful among a ground layer of brambles and bracken but the site is easy to navigate via a number of clearly marked footpaths, some of which link to others through the valley. A surfaced path from the car park provides access for wheelchair users. Elsewhere, paths are prone to mud – so remember your boots.

Park Wood
Keighley
From A650 at Crossflatts follow by-pass. Turn off at roundabout to Thwaites and Worth village. Take first left and cross railway bridge. Follow road into Parkwood Street. Wood is on hillside above Parkwood Street. (SE069409)
14 ha (35 acres)
Bradford Metropolitan Council

While this may not be worth a long-distance trip, if you are in the area, Park Wood is worth a detour.

A pleasant hour or so could be spent strolling through this beech woodland overlooking Keighley and the hills beyond. Evidence of quarrying shows that this hillside was plundered for its gritstone before beech was planted to create the scene you see today.

With fresh green leaves that turn bronze as the days shorten, these woods are best visited in spring and autumn. Little grows on the woodland floor except for patches of heather that thrive in sunnier areas.

This wood could form part of a longer walk over adjacent hills.

MAP 3

Northcliffe Wood
Shipley

From A650 Bradford – Keighley Road take left turn at Frizinghall to Cliff Wood Avenue. The wood is straight ahead. (SE142362)

17 ha (42 acres)

Bradford Metropolitan Council

Follow the high ground at the edge of the woodland to enjoy views to the north towards Shipley and the countryside beyond, and then return along the valley bottom beside a stream for a pleasantly varied circular walk.

The attractive mixed broadleaved woodland of oak, birch, ash, sycamore and beech with holly and elder beneath feels very natural in contrast to other areas that resemble a town park.

Bluebells carpet one area of the woodland in spring accompanied by the song of such summer migrants as chiffchaff and blackcap. The locally rare white hairstreak butterfly has been recorded here and a management programme is now underway to improve its habitat.

Paths are easily followed and some are surfaced which makes this an accessible woodland for the majority of visitors.

Hardcastle Crags
Hebden Bridge

Take A6033 (Keighley Road) north of Hebden Bridge. Turn left into Midgehole Road, follow to the end into National Trust car park. (SD988295)

125 ha (309 acres)

The National Trust

A dramatic landscape and interesting history join forces at Hardcastle Crags to forge an attractive woodland of interest to all ages.

Over the years the steep wooded valley of Hebden Gorge has supported a range of industries – wool from local farms supplied the mill in the valley while charcoal burners provided fuel for local iron smelting.

Today the steep-sided gorge is clothed in beech, sycamore, oak, birch, larch and Scots pine, planted over 150 years. Woodrush, ferns, bracken and bluebells cover the ground where thousands of wood ants rustle through the foliage.

Look out for the slurring stone – a large rock where local children used to slide in their clogs, and an old pannier route which winds up the hillside.

A choice of walks includes the chance to climb the hillside towards Harcastle Crags, the rocky outcrops that give the woods their name. Boots are recommended, particularly for anyone venturing onto the open moors.

Judy Woods
Wyke

From A461 take turning to Norwood Green. Woodland on left, off Station Road. (SE137270) 40 ha (99 acres)

Bradford Metropolitan Council

There is a delightfully rural feel to Judy Woods, a collection of small sites forming an intimate patchwork along the valley of Royds Hall Beck.

The woods sit within a lovely landscape and look more extensive than they are.

They also have a rich social history. Named after Judy North, who lived in a 19th-century cottage near the bridge, they are made up of mixed broadleaves. Ancient woodland was replanted with beech in Victorian times, probably to serve the local mills. Bell pits are lasting reminders of the area's industrial heritage, particularly in Old Hanna Wood.

The beech, stunning in spring and autumn, include some lovely large spreading specimens along with oak and birch areas. Small tributaries of the beck add to the variety and higher ground provides lovely views beneath the canopy.

There are lots of paths and potential circular walks, including a surfaced path suitable for wheelchairs and pushchairs.

MAP 3

Stoneycliffe Wood
Netherton

On the B6117 southwest of
Wakefield, west of village of
Netherton. (SE274161)
40 ha (99 acres)
Yorkshire Wildlife Trust

There is an air of peace about
Stoneycliffe Wood and a host
of interesting features inside.

The woodland clothes the
steep slope down to
Stoneycliffe Beck, which
meanders tortuously along the
valley. Less athletic visitors can
take advantage of benches
provided at intervals
throughout the wood.

Amid this quiet scene a
population of birds thrives –
woodpeckers and summer
warblers among them – with
several rare spider species,
while a small pond supports
ducks and other wildfowl.

Oak and birch dominate this
typical coal measure woodland
though sycamore has taken
hold in some areas and some
lovely gnarled and twisted oak
and sweet chestnut specimens
add to the atmosphere.

Holly, hazel and heather
form the understorey with
bluebells, ramsons, yellow
archangel and several rare
plants, including wood club-
rush, hemlock water droplet
and Sprengels' bramble.

Paths are easy to follow but
those along the valley bottom
can be muddy and slippery –
so boots are recommended.

Bagger Wood
Hood Green

Junction 37 M1 through Dodworth
to Silkstone Common on B6449.
Turn left in Silkstone Common to
Hood Green. Turn right upon
entering Hood Green and follow
the road for about 1.6km (1 mile)
before turning right into the car
park at the western end of the
wood. (SE303026)
27 ha (68 acres)

The Woodland Trust

Just ten minutes from busy
Barnsley, Bagger Wood is a
rural haven enjoyed by around
3,000 visitors every year.

One of a series of steep
hillside woods in an area of
Great Landscape Value, Bagger
and its neighbouring woods

form a distinctive skyline, making a particularly attractive landmark from the nearby village of Dodworth and surrounding area.

The wood, which is part of the South Yorkshire Forest, is well placed for access from several local villages. Visitors can either follow an attractive circular path from the car park or explore the central area via a forest road which is also open to horse riders.

Listed as an ancient woodland site, Bagger Wood was dominated by broadleaves until the 1960s when around half was planted with conifers. Most of the hardwoods that remain – oak, beech and sycamore – date from the 1930s. Today the woodland mix attracts a range

of mammals and sustains a wide variety of flora.

Bagger Wood

South Yorkshire Community Forest

The South Yorkshire Community Forest is a mix of open spaces, woodland, wetland, farmland, meadow and urban areas, covering 153 square miles. The Forest includes the south of

Barnsley, takes in most of Rotherham and the north, south and east of Sheffield. It aims to make access to the countryside easier for all, develop green links to connect the urban areas with the countryside and protect and create areas for wildlife.

MAP 3

Bitholmes Wood
Sheffield
Woodland straddles A6102
Sheffield to Huddersfield road just
north of Oughtibridge and south
of Stocksbridge. (SK293965)
33ha (82acres)
Woodland Trust

Once part of a large hunting
forest and later a focus for
mining, quarrying and industrial
activity, today Bitholmes Wood
is subject to little disturbance.

The semi-natural ancient
woodland lies on steep valley
sides, sandwiched between
Sheffield and the Peak
District National Park and is
home to many bird species,
including woodpeckers and
pied flycatchers.

Limited parking facilities
keep visitor numbers low but
for those who do make it, there
is an attractive circular walk.
Adventurous walkers who
climb to the top end of the
wood are rewarded with fine
views across the Don Valley.

Once a sessile oak woodland
overlooking the valley, the site is
now dominated by sycamore,
although there are still large
areas of ancient mixed
woodland, particularly along
the crags in the upper reaches.

The lower wood still has a
strong ancient woodland feel,
with lots of associated ground
flora, including bluebells, dog's
mercury, wood mellick, wood
millet and cow wheat.

Wharncliffe Woods
Sheffield or Chapeltown
From A61 turn west towards
Grenoside. Take Woodhead Road
north through village. Wood on
left once through village.
(SK324951)
456ha (1127acres)
Forestry Commission

Robust scenery, open
moorland, steep terrain and
streams make a delightful
backdrop for Wharncliffe and
nearby Greno woods – an
enjoyable family outing
destination.

Part of the South Yorkshire
Forest, the woodland has an
interesting history. Wharn is a
corruption of quern, a
handmill used for grinding

grain. In medieval times Wharncliffe Chase was part of a royal hunting park and more recently coal and gannister were mined here. In Greno woods, stone was mined for buildings.

You'll find traces of all these activities in the mix of woodland and fields. Though much of the area was planted with conifers after

World War II, signs of ancient oak and birch woodland are everywhere.

Greno Wood features areas of Corsican pine and extensive heathland with ling, bilberry, broom and gorse. Birch and oak are regenerating here.

All-terrain bikers, horse riders and walkers all get a fair share of access routes, though most are generally strenuous.

Wheata Woods
Sheffield

Follow signs for Grenoside village from A61. Head north out of village along Woodhead Road. (SK328943)
55ha (136 acres)
Sheffield City Council

This attractive site lies on a bus route just 8km (5 miles) north of Sheffield city centre.

The site is made up of three neighbouring woods: Wheata, Prior Royd and Birkin Royd. Part of an extensive wooded area, these are distinctive from other local woods, being largely semi-natural ancient woodland.

Rich in ground flora, wildlife and bird species, it has been designated a local nature reserve. Much is also a scheduled ancient monument, featuring the remains of a Romano-British settlement.

Wheata Wood, the largest of the three, is open, flat and easy to access, even with wheelchairs. Prior Royd is a denser wood with more steep slopes, while Birkin Royd clothes the steep sides of a stream valley and is the most difficult to access.

While oak and birch trees dominate, you'll also discover alder in the wetter areas plus beech, sweet chestnut, sycamore and conifers.

MAP 3

Snake Woodlands
Glossop
Take A57 from Glossop or
Sheffield. Park in Birchin Clough
lay-by. (SK109915)
152ha (376acres) AONB
Forestry Commission

Woodland trails lead down
steep-sided valleys through
spruce and larch plantations.
The best of these follow the
river which brings welcome
variety to an otherwise
conifer-dominated site.

There are some pleasant
glades along the river with one
leading through an open valley
of moorland vegetation where
you can enjoy a picnic and
the views.

Walking is generally easy-to-
moderate but the steps from the
road to the start of the trails are
fairly steep and care should be
taken on the stone-surfaced path,
which can get slippery when
wet. The blue trail will take
around one-and-a-half hours, the
white trail an hour. Likely to get
muddy after rain, it's best to go
armed with wellingtons.

Snake Woodlands can form
part of a longer walk to Kinder
Scout, the highest peak in the
National Park.

Shire Hill
Glossop
From Glossop take A57 Snake
Pass. Turn left before leaving
Glossop into Woodcock Grove
signposted Pyegrove Estate and
Shire Hill. Follow road to car park
and footpath leading to wood.
(SK048944)
30ha (73acres) AONB
**Peak District National
Park Authority**

Shire Hill is something of a
tranquil gem in the heart of an
urban area. A drive through a
housing estate to a car park and
children's play area is followed
by a walk across a football field
and then up a steep, uneven
narrow path on the edge of
another housing estate.

But once you enter the
wood, the environment quickly
changes, for this ancient
woodland of birch and oak has
a lovely atmosphere,
particularly when bathed in
afternoon sun. Trees cover the

side of the hill and it feels safe and quiet, ideal for local walks or a short visit after crossing the Pennines. The Trans-Pennine cycle route runs to the north of the wood along the Roman road and links to the Pennine Way.

Tracks and small paths meander through the wood, drawing you to the top of the hill where the landscape changes to heathland, with fine views.

Tom Wood
Glossop

Take A626 between Glossop and Hollingworth towards Charlesworth. Wood is off Woodseats Lane. (SJ998930)
11ha (28acres)

Woodland Trust

The steep terrain and largely undeveloped character of Tom Wood make it a rewarding place to explore – with care – and a great destination for those seeking a morning or afternoon trip to the countryside.

The reward is a beautiful landscape with ash, oak, birch and sycamore, often balanced with a good display of varied wild flowers.

The woodland has a truly rural feel, lining the steep sides of a large bowl-shaped valley in the heart of flat farmland. It forms a clear landmark from the surrounding villages, hills and roads, making it a little surprising given that Manchester is very close by.

The steep slopes can become very muddy so sturdy footwear should be worn, whatever the time of year.

MAP 3

Longdendale Estate
Stalybridge

From A57 in Glossop, take B6105
and follow road alongside
reservoirs to car park and
National Park information centre
at Torside. (SK008975)
6551ha (16190acres) AONB
United Utilities

A small corner of the vast
Longdendale Estate, the
fairytale quality of Wildboar
Clough makes it a wonderful
place to take children. Here
you'll find a remnant of the
oak and birch woodland that
once covered much of the
Peak District.

Something of a rarity, the
woodland is particularly
interesting as well as attractive,
with a path winding uphill
between stunted oaks and
boulders while a small stream
cascades down the rock-strewn
ravine. It is a great place to
explore and enjoy the views
across the reservoirs and
moorlands beyond.

Within the small and quickly
explored woodland there are
more open areas, which add to
the interest.

Entry is via the well-surfaced
Longendale Trail, part of the
Trans-Pennine Trail, which is
suitable for wheelchair use
although the woodland itself
is not. The woodland path
climbs up the site of the
clough to an open moor
where vegetation includes
bracken, heather and bilberry.
The route is not difficult but
boots are recommended.

Towneley Woods
Burnley

Follow signs from M65 & A671 for
Towneley Hall Park. (SD855307)
20 ha (49 acres)
Burnley Borough Council

Woodland has existed in the
grounds of historic Towneley
Hall since 1400 but the
visitor's route is along paths
laid out in the 1800s when the
grounds were landscaped in
classic English style.

The legacy of this historical
background can be enjoyed
among the mixed native
broadleaves and exotic species
that populate the site today.
Look for sculptures created

along the walks here and at nearby Grove Lane Plantations, Padiham and in the woods of Gawthorpe Hall.

Towering beech trees are a feature of this woodland. The many other surprises waiting to be discovered include relics from the 19th century such as an arched passageway in Thanet Lee Wood, a ha-ha, rustic tunnels and the Monks Well grotto.

The woodland itself is a mixture of exotic and native trees. Soil changes throughout the site are reflected in the variety of ground flora – clay-loving ramson in some sections contrasting with an abundance of bluebells in more acidic areas.

Additional woods to visit

Woods shown on the western edge of Map 3 are featured in Exploring Woodland Guide to The North West and The Lakes. These include:

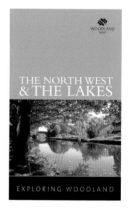

Cuerden Valley Park
Phillips Park
Beacon Fell Country Park
Spring Wood
Strinesdale Countryside Area
Tandle Hill Country Park
Elnup Wood
Haigh Hall
Heaton Park
Grove Lane Plantations
Lever Park
Roddlesworth &
  Tockholes Woods
Blackley Forest
High Shores Clough Woodland
Jumbles Country Park
Raveden Wood,
  Smithills Hall Estate
Walker Fold Woodlands
Wilderswood
Gisburn Forest
Borsdane Wood
Hagg Wood

MAP 4

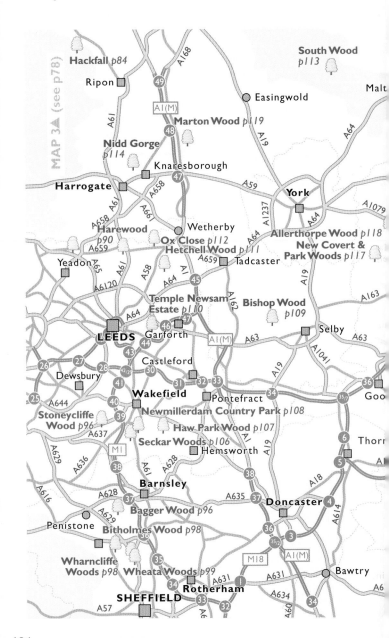

South Wood *p113*

Hackfall *p84*

Ripon

49

A168

Malt

Easingwold

MAP 3▲ (see p78)

A1(M)

48 Marton Wood *p119*

A19

A61

Nidd Gorge *p114*

A64

Knaresborough

47

A658

A59

York

Harrogate

A658

A61

A64

A1237

A1079

A66

A658 A61

Harewood *p90*

Wetherby

Allerthorpe Wood *p118*

A659

Ox Close *p112*
Hetchell Wood *p111*

New Covert &
Park Woods *p117*

Yeadon

A64

A659

Tadcaster

A65 A61

A6120

A58

A1

A19

A163

45

Temple Newsam
Estate *p110*

A64

A162

Bishop Wood *p109*

A161

46

47

Selby

LEEDS

Garforth

A1(M)

A63

A63

44

43

Castleford

A1041

26

27

28

42/23

A19

36

Dewsbury

30

31

32 33

35/1

Goo

25

41

Wakefield

Pontefract

34

A644

40

Newmillerdam Country Park *p108*

A629

39

Stoneycliffe
Wood *p96*

Haw Park Wood *p107*

6

Thor

A637

Seckar Woods *p106*

A19

5

A636

38

A61

A628

Hemsworth

A18

A

38

A629

M1

A16

A635

37

Doncaster

4

A616

A628

37

Barnsley

A614

Bagger Wood *p96*

A629

36

Penistone

Bitholmes Wood *p98*

35/2

3

36

A1(M)

Wharncliffe
Woods *p98*

35

Wheata Woods *p99*

M18

Bawtry

A631

A631

34

Rotherham

A634

A6

SHEFFIELD

33

32

A60

34

A57

A6

A64
A1039
A169

MAP 2 ▲ (see p48)

A165

10 miles

10 km

Flamborough
Head

N

■ Bridlington

A614

Driffield ●

A163

A164

A165

 cklington

Market
eighton ●

A1079

Beverley ●

■

A165

A1034

Little Wold
ntation p120

A164

KINGSTON UPON HULL

A63 Nut Wood,
Wauldby Scrogs &
Constantine Wood p120

A63

Hessle ●

Withernsea ●

A1033

R. Humber

Barton-
upon-
Humber ●

A1077

A160

A15

Immingham ■

A180

Scunthorpe
■

⑤

Grimsby ■

A46

A1173

Cleethorpes ■

3

M180

④

A1084

A18

A1031

A159

Brigg ●

A15

Caistor ●

A16

insborough

A1103

Market
Rasen ●

A631

A46

A631

Louth ■

MAP 4

Seckar Woods
Newmillerdam

Car park signposted from A61
Barnsley to Wakefield. Turn down
Seckar Lane. (SE326143)
48 ha (119 acres) SSSI

**Wakefield Metropolitan
District Council**

One of only five locations
designated Sites of Special
Scientific Interest in Wakefield,
Seckar Wood is a delightful

place to visit, with lots of variety
and several interesting habitats.

A 'must' for any visitor to
Newmillerdam Country Park
(see page 108), neighbouring
Seckar Wood is a local nature
reserve with woodland, wet and
dry heath and some rare plants.

Within the woods are the
remains of a summerhouse and
a series of ponds – part of a
never-to-be-completed
landscape plan by photographer
Warner Gothard who bought
the wood in the 1920s.

Modern-day owners
Wakefield Metropolitan District
Council recently opened up
areas of water to attract
amphibians and dragonflies.

Thin soils that developed
over the bare sandstone left
from former mine workings
now support gorse, heather
and wavy hair grass that has
created a distinctive habitat
and open landscape – an
attractive contrast to the rather
dense woodland.

Seckar Woods

Haw Park Wood
Wintersett

A638 heading south, turn right signposted to Crofton opposite Crofton Arms public house. Follow tourist signs to Wintersett village. After Anglers Retreat public house, turn right. Car park is 800m on right. (SE375154)

65 ha (161 acres)

Wakefield Metropolitan District Council

One of the main draws to Haw Park Wood is its heronry but this is just one of many interesting features throughout the estate.

A network of footpaths and bridleways provides quiet, peaceful, easy walking with benches and occasional sculptures along the way.

Areas of dense larch and pine were planted to provide pit props for local coal mines but many are being replaced with broadleaved species to attract more wildlife. There are also mature oak trees and young birch, typical of coal measure woodland.

The Barnsley Canal passes through the southern part of the wood. Opened in 1799 to carry coal from Barnsley and grain from Wakefield, it is no longer navigable. Today it provides a habitat for frogs, waterplants and several species of dragonfly.

Further information available at the Waterton Countryside Discovery Centre.

MAP 4

Newmillerdam
Country Park
Newmillerdam

Follow A61 south to
Newmillerdam. Follow brown
tourist sign to Newmillerdam
Country Park. (SE331157)
95 ha (235 acres)
**Wakefield Metropolitan
District Council**

Once part of the Pilkington
family's Chevet Estate,
Newmillerdam Country Park is
a lovely combination of lake and
peaceful broadleaved woodland.

For many, the lake is the
main attraction. There is a
causeway across the water and
a well-surfaced path follows a
circular route around the lake
– providing easy access for
wheelchairs and pushchairs.

The route offers plenty of
interest, from viewing wildfowl
on the lake to exploration of
the woods of oak, sweet
chestnut and some fine mature
beech. They are populated by a
plethora of birdlife – tree
creepers, woodpeckers and
owls included.

Newmillerdam Country Park

The woods south and west of the lake are the quieter parts of the country park. Stands of pine and larch, planted in the 1950s, are being thinned to make way for oak, ash, birch and hazel which will encourage more wildlife. Bluebells grow in the southern woodland.

It is worth combining a visit here with neighbouring Seckar Wood (see page 106).

Bishop Wood
Cawood

5km (3 miles) west of Selby and 5km (3 miles) south of Cawood. On B1222 midway between Sherburn and Cawood.
(SE561333)
330 ha (816 acres)
Forestry Commission

A former ancient woodland oasis in an agriculture-dominated landscape, Bishop Wood creates an immediate impression of size.

It is easy to get the idea that this is a relatively new wood, thanks to an extensive post-war planting programme by the Forestry Commission. Scots and Corsican pine, spruce and poplar are regularly harvested and replanted.

Native wet woodland species including alder, willow, birch and hazel are colonising along the many streams that line the site. Dotted about the main woodland are small groups of mature oak and ash. In the southern part of the wood, a sensitive programme of work is under way to re-establish native species such as oak, ash, hazel, alder and birch.

Access is via a range of routes but since there is no waymarking, it is worth taking a map and compass. There are ample stone rides, enabling less-abled access but the minor paths off the main grid can be muddy.

MAP 4

Temple Newsam Estate

Temple Newsam Estate
Whitkirk

M1 J64. Follow Selby Road A63
west towards Leeds. Turn left into
Colton Rd. Continue along this
road, turning right into The Elm
Walk. Wood is on left. (SE360320)
157 ha (388 acres)
Leeds City Council

Dubbed 'the Hampton Court
of the North', Temple Newsam
Estate has the makings of a
great family day out, whatever
the weather.

Just minutes from Leeds, this
is a country park with knobs on
– a combination of formal
gardens, lakeside and riverside
walks, secluded spots and
masses of public space to
enjoy football, athletics, golf
and play facilities. There is also
a working farm, museum and
rare breeds centre.

Mostly planted in the early
18th century, large areas were
used as a deer park and today it
forms part of the Forest of Leeds.

The name reveals the origins
of the estate, which was granted
to the Knights Templar in 1155.
Capability Brown's influence

can be seen in mature areas of woodland such as Avenue Woods. The estate's deserted medieval village of Colton features veteran oaks dating back 600 years or more.

Both standing and fallen timber provide a rich habitat for invertebrates, birds, mosses and fungi.

Hetchell Wood
Thorner

Approaching from Wetherby on A58, at East Rigton turn left signposted Thorner. Keep left at triangular intersection (Milner Lane). Reserve entrance on left after 800m. (SE380422)
11 ha (27 acres) SSSI
Bramham Estates

Don't be deceived by your first glimpse of Hetchell Wood. It may look insignificant, but this is a treasure trove of discovery – a mix of limestone grassland, semi-natural broadleaved woodland and alder carr that unfolds its secrets one by one.

A beech knoll surrounding the old limestone quarry gives way to cleared thorn thicket supporting rock rose, dyers greenweed and salad burnet where Hebridean sheep graze.

An outcrop of gritstone at Hetchell Crags offers wonderful views across a patchwork of fields and copses with glimpses of Barsey Beck. But parents should beware of the precarious drop.

The well-surfaced path leads down the slope through dappled shade, with hazel and holly and small groups of crab apple and rowan. The underwood is coppiced to encourage invertebrates and a variety of insects can be seen and heard.

At the beck, where spring meadowsweet gives off its subtle scent, a footbridge, stiles and gates have been built to improve access.

MAP 4

Ox Close
East Keswick

At Boston Spa exit on A1 take A659 west. 2km (1.5 miles) after Collingham village, turn left signposted East Keswick, car park at junction. Cross road on foot to bridleway. (SE364459)
14 ha (35 acres)
East Keswick Wildlife Trust

Not the easiest wood to find but Ox Close is worth a little effort. For this site – popular with local residents – has much of interest to keep visitors intrigued.

Standing on the edge of the River Wharfe Valley and larger than neighbouring Hetchell Wood, Ox Close Wood is explored via a meandering circular path.

The most accessible areas were cleared 11 years ago but vigorous regeneration of ash, elm, birch and sycamore has left the area rich and dense. Look out for occasional mature larch and pine.

Further along the path, sycamore is more common and scrub is being removed to make way for limestone grassland, encouraged by grazing Hebridean sheep and the occasional goat. This is a working wood – with two kilns producing charcoal and adding another layer of interest. Rest a while on the recently installed woodland seats by the kilns.

On leaving, it is worth pausing on the robust green footbridge over the River Wharfe to enjoy the fine valley views, explore the banks for signs of crayfish, otters, kingfishers, breeding goosanders and grey wagtails or enjoy a picnic.

South Wood
Hovingham

From Malton take B1257 west. At Hovingham sign turn left, wood is 1.5km (1 mile) on left. (SE660740)

William Worsley

 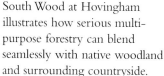

South Wood at Hovingham illustrates how serious multi-purpose forestry can blend seamlessly with native woodland and surrounding countryside.

The estate takes its forestry seriously, producing high quality timber. That is good news for visitors since it produces an interesting balance of stability and change from an array of species in various stages of maturity. It also provides great views across the surrounding hills.

Spruce, Scots pine, larch, beech, oak, sweet chestnut and sycamore make up the woodland mix, blending harmoniously with surrounding woods – Fryton, Wath, Slingsby Banks and Conesthorpe Bank.

As the woods are used for sporting activities visitors are asked to keep to public rights of way and well-surfaced rides. Mature oaks feature at key points in the wood, including the ridges and there is a magnificent stand of beech near the bridleway, which links a series of earthworks.

The eastern end of South Wood is bounded by Wath Beck, where alder and willow provide dappled shade for wetland plant and insect communities.

MAP 4

Nidd Gorge

Harrogate

From Knaresborough travel along the B6165 towards Ripley for approx 2km (just over a mile). The road follows alongside a woodland. At the end of the wood take first turning left which leads to a small car park. (SE328579)

62 ha (153 acres) SSSI

The Woodland Trust

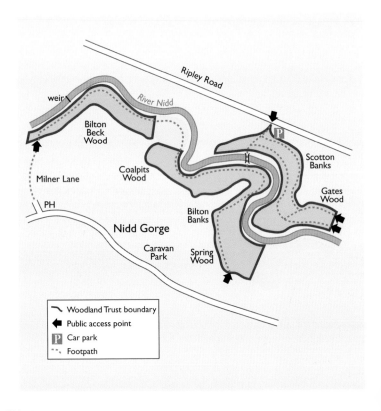

Nidd Gorge

Acres of broadleaf woodland brimming with wildlife adorn the steep cliffs and slopes of Yorkshire's stunning Nidd Gorge.

Nestling between Harrogate and Knaresborough, the woodland, which dates back to at least 1600, is actually made up of five woods: Coalpits Wood, Bilton Banks, Spring Wood, Scotton Banks and Gates Wood.

A local conservation site, the valley woodlands and the surrounding agricultural land are a magnet for local residents, walkers and fishermen. All are drawn to a landscape sculpted by the River Nidd whose waters have rushed around the rocky bends and shallows of this imposing landmark since the last Ice Age when it cut a deep gorge through the soft sandstone.

History has left its mark on Nidd Gorge. At Gates Hill, in the Scotton Banks section of the woodland, now overgrown, is a defensive earthwork where local legend says Colonel Fairfax mounted defence cannon for the siege of Knaresborough during the Civil War. Coalpits Wood, south of the river, retains the

MAP 4

Bilton Beck

remnants of bell pits where coal was once excavated.

Most of the oak woods on the Nidd's southern banks had been cleared by World War ll and the area is now dominated by broadleaf coppice regrowth, and some regenerating sycamore though the area still has a natural feel to it. The northern bank is a mixture of conifers and broadleaves.

Today the gorge nurtures more than 80 species of birds and 30 different kinds of mammals, reptiles and amphibians. Bats, roe deer, tawny owls, herons, and spotted and green woodpeckers are just some of the inhabitants of the five woods.

Ninety-one species of fungi have been identified in the gorge including puffballs, cup fungi, jelly and bracket fungi. There are numerous plants and flowers, which can only be found in ancient woodland, among them nine species of fern, dog's mercury, wild garlic and bluebells.

Bilton Beck & Rudding Bottoms
Knaresborough/Harrogate

Follow directions as for Nidd Gorge. These woods are an extension of Nidd Gorge. (SE307583)

17 ha (42 acres)

The Woodland Trust

New Covert & Park Woods

Melbourne

From York follow the B1228 (York–Howden) through the villages of Elvington and Sutton upon Derwent. Just past the turning to Melbourne where the road turns south, a car park can be found approximately 800m from the junction down a short track approximately 20m into wood. (SE732442)

8 ha (21 acres)

The Woodland Trust

These linked woods provide a quiet retreat.

Their isolation keeps visitor numbers low and wildlife interest high. But the visitor is well catered for with a car park, information board and over a mile of footpaths.

A circular route from the car park leads through a newly planted area, past a pond into New Covert, a wet woodland dominated by birch with willow and alder, and into a clearing – a favourite haunt for barn owls at twilight. Old ditches beside the path mark the wood's boundaries as well as providing drainage.

New Covert is linked to Park Wood via a thicket of willow and alder on the edge of a glade, where willow tits can sometimes be heard. Park Wood is precious ancient woodland, dominated by birch where gnarled oak trees provide a haven for wildlife. Volunteers have been installing footbridges, clearing paths and removing rhododendron to give native flowers a chance.

117

MAP 4

Allerthorpe Wood
Barmby Moor

Head north on A1079 towards
Barmby Moor. Take left after turn
for Barmby Moor opposite garage
into Sutton Lane. Wood is approx
2.5km (1.5 miles) on left.
(SE753479)
148 ha (366 acres)

Forestry Commission

If you're looking for a moody,
misty place to get to grips with
Nature, try a walk around
Allerthope Wood, particularly
in the winter months.

   This sheltered wood is
popular with local residents,
and dog owners in particular,
since there are few other local
areas of open access land.

   There are many walks,
including an extensive all-
weather surfaced ride network,
leading through the plantation.
The land is flat, well drained
and dominated with Scots pine
although the site is fringed
with birch and a scattering of
oaks. Willow can also be found
in wetter ground.

   The open ground has been
colonised by gorse, holly and
birch. Some areas where
conifers have been removed
will remain unplanted to allow
heather to re-colonise.

   The wood's southern
boundary abuts the modern
stables at Thornton House
Farm where a bridleway
provides a link through to
Allerthope. It's also worth
combining a visit here with a
trip to nearby Weldrake Wood
or simply to enjoy the views
across the Yorkshire Wolds.

Marton Wood
Marton

Exit junction 47 or 48 of A1(M) onto A168, signed Marton-cum-Grafton. In Marton village turn sharp right into Church Lane. Cross junction into Legram Lane, wood on left. (SE420617)

7 ha (17 acres)

North Yorkshire County Council

A convenient place to break a long journey on the A1. Pick up picnic ingredients from the village store, follow the attractive country lane with its ivy-clad mature hedgerow oaks and soak up the tranquillity that this small oak woodland has to offer.

The change in underlying soil creates a wood of contrasting character. Look for drainage ditches in the low-lying sections and you'll know you're on clay. Head west and you'll find well-spaced beech trees towering above buckler fern which thrive in the lighter and better-drained conditions found here.

As well as a public footpath running through the wood there is also an informal circular walk. Paths used by horse riders can turn muddy after rain.

Pheasant feeding troughs suggest the tranquillity may occasionally be broken during the shooting season.

MAP 4

Little Wold Plantation
South Cave

Turn off A63 to South Cave. In
South Cave turn right into
Beverley Road and after 400m
turn left into Little Wold Lane.
Roadside parking normally available
here. Little Wold Plantation can be
seen on hillside and found by
walking along road, which turns
into bridle track before reaching
wood. (SE931323)
5 ha (13 acres)
The Woodland Trust

While little is known about the
history of Little Wold
Plantation, this attractive
mature woodland has
established itself as a favourite
among walkers in the
Yorkshire Wolds.

The wood can be reached
from the popular Wolds Way
long-distance footpath which
skims its southern boundary.
Here, walkers can enjoy
commanding views across a
largely agricultural scene.

Beech and ash are dominant
with a smattering of sycamore.
What is striking on a tour of
the woodland is the vibrant
regeneration that is developing
beneath the canopy of trees.

Rich in birdlife, Little Wold
Plantation also supports large
colonies of deadly nightshade –
rare in this region.

Situated on the edge of the
Wolds, its elevated position offers
commanding views across the
Vale of York from the western
boundary and across the Humber
estuary to North Lincolnshire
when viewing to the south.

Nut Wood, Wauldby Scrogs & Constantine Woods
Cottingham, Humberside

From Humber Bridge roundabout
with the A63 head north for about
3.5km (2 miles) up A164 past a
roundabout before turning left on
the road to Melton. Take first
turning right on the road to South
Cave and follow for about 1.6km
(1 mile) until road takes a long
bend in front of Raywell House on
the right. Opposite on left is
entrance to Constantine Wood
where roadside parking can
normally be found. (SE991304)
14 ha (35 acres)
The Woodland Trust

Woodland is a precious resource in East Yorkshire where cover has dwindled to just 1.9 per cent. But what the county lacks in quantity it makes up for in quality at Nut Wood and Wauldby Scrogs, known locally as the Bluebell Wood.

This provides a welcome oasis in a largely arable landscape, well loved and used by local people. Parts of the woodland date from the 13th century and have a rich ground flora of dog's mercury,

wood anemone, wild garlic and bluebells.

Neighbouring Constantine Wood – a baby in comparison – was created in 1999 as part of the Woodland Trust's Woods on your Doorstep community wood to extend and buffer the ancient woodland.

In this delightful setting more than 36 bird species, 80 types of plant, 20 insect and 10 fungus species thrive – as does man, who can choose from a series of circular walks or longer walks through the site.

Nut Wood

WOODLAND
TRUST

Trees and forests are crucial to life on our planet. They generate oxygen, play host to a spectacular variety of wildlife and provide us with raw materials and shelter. They offer us tranquillity, inspire us and refresh our souls.

Founded in 1972, the Woodland Trust is now the UK's leading woodland conservation charity. By acquiring sites and campaigning for woodland it aims to conserve, restore and re-establish native woodland to its former glory. The Trust now owns and cares for over 1,100 woods throughout the UK.

The Woodland Trust wants to see:
no further loss of ancient woodland
the variety of woodland wildlife restored and improved
an increase in new native woodland
an increase in people's understanding and enjoyment of woodland

The Woodland Trust has in excess of 170,000 members who share this vision. For every new member, the Trust can care for approximately half an acre of native woodland. For details of how to join the Woodland Trust please either ring FREEPHONE 0800 026 9650 or visit the website at www.woodland-trust.org.uk.

If you have enjoyed the woods in this book please consider leaving a legacy to the Woodland Trust. Legacies of all sizes play an invaluable role in helping the Trust to create new woodland and secure precious ancient woodland threatened by development and destruction. For further information please either call 01476 581129 or visit our dedicated website at www.legacies.org.uk

Letah Wood

Further Information

Public transport

Each entry gives a brief description of location, nearest town and grid reference. Traveline provides impartial journey planning information about all public transport services either by ringing 0870 608 2608 (calls charged at national rates) or visit www.traveline.org.uk. For information about the Sustrans National Cycle Network either ring 0117 929 0888 or visit www.sustrans.org.uk

Useful contacts

Forestry Commission, 0845 367 3787, www.forestry.gov.uk
National Trust, 0870 458 4000, www.nationaltrust.org.uk
Wildlife Trusts, 0870 036 7711, www.wildlifetrusts.org
RSPB, 01767 680551, www.rspb.org.uk
Royal Forestry Society, 01442 822028, www.rfs.org.uk
Tree Council, 020 7407 9992, www.treecouncil.org.uk
National Forest, 01283 551211, www.nationalforest.org
Woodland Trust, 01476 581111, www.woodland-trust.org.uk

Recommend a Wood

You can play a part in helping us complete this series. We are inviting readers to nominate a wood or woods they think should be included. We are interested in any woodland with public access in the UK.

To recommend a wood please photocopy this page and provide as much of the following information as possible:

About the wood

Name of wood: _____

Nearest town: _____

Approximate size: _____ ha/acres

Owner/manager: _____

A few words on why you think it should be included:

_____

_____

About you

Your name: _____

Your postal address: _____

_____

_____ Post code: _____

If you are a member of the Woodland Trust please provide your membership number. [   ]

Please send to: Exploring Woodland Guides, The Woodland Trust, Autumn Park, Dysart Road, Grantham, Lincolnshire NG31 6LL, by fax on 01476 590808 or e-mail woodlandguides@woodland-trust.org.uk

Thank you for your help

Other Guides in the Series

Chilterns to the
Welsh Borders

The South West
of England

The South East
of England

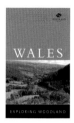

Wales

The Peak District
& Central England

East Anglia &
North Thames

The North West
& The Lakes

Coming soon
Scotland

If you would like to be notified when certain titles are due for
publication please either write to Exploring Woodland Guides,
The Woodland Trust, Autumn Park, Dysart Road, Grantham,
Lincolnshire NG31 6LL or e-mail woodlandguides@woodland-
trust.org.uk

Index